The Money Anxiety CURE

A Path to Financial Wellness

D0838822

Koorosh Ostowari

For further information on this book, workshops, classes and speaking engagements, you can contact Koorosh at:

koorosh@themoneyanxietycure.com

You can also connect with Koorosh here:

Website: TheMoneyAnxietyCure.com

Facebook: facebook.com/PersonalProsperityToday

Twitter: twitter.com/MindfulMoney1

ISBN 978-1-939116-36-9

Published by Waterfront Digital Press
2055 Oxford Avenue
Cardiff, CA 92007

The
Money Anxiety
CURE

A Path to Financial Wellness

Koorosh Ostowari

WATERFRONT DIGITAL PRESS

Table of Contents

INTRODUCTION

The Dalai Lama, when asked what surprised him most about humanity, answered:

Man. Because he sacrifices his health in order to make money. Then he sacrifices money to recuperate his health. And then he is so anxious about the future that he does not enjoy the present; the result being that he does not live in the present or the future; he lives as if he is never going to die, and then he dies having never really lived.

In fall 2008, the US economy almost dropped off the map. The real estate market tanked, the stock market lost almost half its value, families lost homes, retirees lost their 401Ks, and two trillion dollars seemed to vanish into thin air. In an instant, we all learned the same lesson: fortunes can be lost overnight. It was a huge shock to our collective system to witness the impermanence of the money we worked so hard for, but it was also a great lesson. No matter how mindful and attentive we are—managing, balancing, living frugally, investing wisely—there are no guarantees.

Uncertainty creates anxiety, and we are engaged in a modern collective anxiety known as money anxiety disorder. Money anxiety disorder lies at the heart of so many of the disruptions that occur in our lives, our society, and our world. It can be triggered by events like fluctuations in the marketplace, loss of a job, having to ask for a raise, enduring a divorce, or struggling to stay on budget. Like the economy itself, our anxiety about money fluctuates. But we don't have to be at the mercy of it. We can learn to cope with unpredictable financial times and stop the panic. There is a cure for money anxiety disorder.

The first step to the cure is to get a handle on the practical ins and outs of your money management. Learning how to budget, set financial goals, create a system for paying bills, and plan wisely for retirement are crucial pragmatic tactics that we all must learn if we are to experience peace and security around money. There are thousands of books about money management. I highly advise picking one up and learning the nuts and bolts of managing your money.

This book, however, will not offer you advice on accounting, budgeting, spreadsheets, or numbers. Instead, we'll focus on a deeper cure: how to change your attitude toward money and create a realistic and balanced definition of your own personal prosperity. Using mindfulness, reflective journaling, and somatic tools, you'll learn to better manage your anxiety around money—and your life.

So many of us were raised to believe that financial success and material prosperity are the most important things we can aspire to in our lives. But where does that leave us when things don't go well with our bank accounts, when we don't achieve what we think we should have achieved when we expected to achieve it, or worse, when we make a lot of money and experience professional success only to realize we are still not happy? And when the entire world seems to be in an economic downturn, does that mean that we too are doomed to misery?

In times of uncertainty and unease, it is possible to be at peace with your financial situation and your lot in life. This book was written from my experiences teaching Money & Mindfulness courses to individuals in my community who run the gamut from rich to poor but share a common a desire to find peace and fulfillment in their lives. I also teach these financial mindfulness programs to prisoners in California jails whose incarceration mirrors the trapped feelings that so many of my students express, regardless of their actual circumstances. Through my work with hundreds of students, I've noticed that they all exhibit a slavery to fear which keeps them from being truly prosperous in the most meaningful sense.

The goal of this book is to help you cure your money anxiety disorder and create a positive and powerful personal definition of prosperity that is achievable for you. Using the age-old tools of mindfulness meditation and somatic practices as well as real, practical advice, I'll teach you a different perspective on your current financial status and help you to envision a future that is in line with your skills, your values, and yes, your dreams. This book is not about getting rich quick. Rather, it's a guide to creating true and lasting contentment in every aspect of your life, starting right where you are in this very moment.

I ask you to pause for a moment and ask yourself a few initial questions:

- What is your personal definition of prosperity?

- What is your unique gift to this world?

- Are your job, lifestyle, and current financial situation helping you to realize your goals?

- Or are they obstacles that prevent you from experiencing true financial, creative, and spiritual freedom?

- Is anxiety about money a barrier to your ability to be content with your life?

You can take charge of your own financial life. More importantly, you can learn to show up with courage and conviction, and in so doing, become embodied with positive change that will inspire others and make a difference in this world. Regardless of your current job, financial situation, or social status, you can learn how to shine your brilliance now. This book will teach you how.

Imprisoned by Fear, Anxiety, and Worry

What lies behind us and what lies ahead of us are tiny matters compared to what lies within us.

—*Ralph Waldo Emerson*

I have had the opportunity to work with so many people struggling on their path, including inmates within the California penal system who have particularly helped me to distill my program to its most potent elements. Those I work with in the jails come from all walks of life: rich, poor, blue collar, white collar, and all types of racial backgrounds. They have one thing in common: an inability to manage their stress productively, which led them to the position they are in now. As a result of their choices, they were caught up in a variety of clever schemes and strategies to escape, numb out, or deny their pain with some combination of cheating, lying, stealing, or drug use.

The good news is that once caught and incarcerated, many of these prisoners come to my classes ready to consider a new way to live. They are open to learning new ways of managing the fears, stressors, and issues that influence their actions regarding money. They are ready to begin the humbling process of filling up their spiritual bank accounts first. They come to mindfulness meditation to learn how to build a foundation for their new home.

Those in jail have a sense of urgency for getting started on a new path. Their past behaviors have depleted them in so many ways. But their situations are really just a microcosm of what we are all going through in this country. We're all prisoners of our own fears and our unhealthy attitudes toward money, success, and happiness. What I teach prisoners and what I teach those outside the prison walls is the same.

My Story

I arrived in the US from Iran as a teenager in 1973. Like most immigrants, I have always felt a tremendous motivation to succeed and prosper. I come from a lineage of successful real estate dealers, land owners, traders, and merchants. I was fortunate enough to have had a good business sense from a very young age because I was exposed to the wheeling and dealing of the adults around me. Coming to America was a chance for me to become rich and successful and to cultivate a deeper understanding of business, economics, and financial security.

From a young age, I was conditioned to be ambitious about making money. I entered the real estate business when I was eighteen, and I was so successful that I was able to retire at age thirty-five. At that point, I spent several years immersing myself in Buddhist studies, attending retreats, and exploring deeper insight about how to create balance, peace, and abundance in my life. Learning the age-old Buddhist practices helped me cultivate deeper insight and skillfulness in attaining and maintaining a prosperous life on many levels. Especially helpful were the Buddhist principles of mindfulness, compassion, equanimity, generosity, balanced effort, concentration, right speech, and clarity of intention. These practices helped me release old, deeply engrained habits of greed, jealousy, lack, fear, and a need to win at any cost.

Despite my early financial success, it wasn't until my midthirties that I began to have a truly balanced and prosperous life—when I felt I had enough money to stop working and devote myself fulltime to awakening and liberating the other areas of my life. Until that point, I could sense how even with enough money, free time, and leisure, I was not fully at peace, happy, or content. I needed to stop and try to understand what was going on inside of me through deeper inquiry and insight. In some ways I sought to replenish my karmic bank account, or to at least dedicate my sincere effort to awakening parts of me that were closed, confused, and lost in anger and hatred. Of course, this has been an ongoing process that never ends.

Through sincere dedication, commitment, and effort, I believe that everyone can come to a place of balanced and sustainable prosperity. Through my years of teaching courses on mindfulness and money to prisoners and those lacking in resources in my community, I have seen time and again how adopting practices of mindfulness and developing somatic (body-based) awareness about money helps create a true sense of prosperity—one that encompasses all of the areas of life in which one can and should feel rich: not just financially and in one's career, but also in personal relationships, physical health, creative expression, community and the impact one's life has on this world.

In writing about the cure for money anxiety disorder, I draw from my over thirty years as a professional businessman, twenty-five years of Buddhist meditation and mindfulness practice, and my training in somatics and embodiment practices. I also draw from the experience and wisdom of others around the topic of prosperity: I interviewed dozens of folks from all walks of life on how they experience prosperity in their own lives. The wisdom and skillful means that led many of these folks to experience a sustained level of prosperity and balance was very moving. So I included some of their stories in this book because I feel it is critical to draw and learn from the wisdom of people who have so many unique ways of experiencing prosperity. I felt blessed and touched by the journey of each individual that I interviewed. I believe their willingness to express what was useful and supportive on their journeys can give us invaluable insight into what prosperity truly is.

You can also get insight as to what is *not* a prosperous way of living by seeing and learning from the pain and suffering of others. Unresolved negative habits, conditioning, and fear increase the likelihood of financial and spiritual poverty, even if on the surface it is tempting to get caught in the notion that a flashy, materialistic life is the same thing as prosperity.

Our lives are interconnected, and the peace, joy, and prosperity of others can inspire our own lives (and vice versa, of course). The Dalai Lama said: "If you want to be prosperous, make sure your neighbor is prosperous as well."

Mindfulness Meditation and Somatic Practices

In my Mindfulness & Money courses and throughout this book, I draw attention to the practice of mindfulness meditation, which comes from Buddhism in the East, and somatic practices, which help us tune in to how we are feeling in our bodies and how that relates to our anxiety and fears about money and life.

Mindfulness meditation is a concept that can seem daunting and esoteric at first. For us in the West, the concept of "sitting still and doing nothing" is counterintuitive to what we have been taught our entire lives: to be productive, ambitious, and always in motion. Even when we are sitting still, it's often because we are distracting ourselves with television, food, or sleeping. This is not to say that television, food, and sleeping are bad things or that we should avoid them. Quite the contrary. Food and sleeping are absolutely necessary elements of our lives—and television can have its place, too. But mindfulness meditation means that we also make room for another kind of sitting still: the kind where we gain insight into our own minds and habits and ways of being.

Mindfulness meditation is extremely easy to learn. I have never, in all my years of teaching this work, encountered a student who could not get the hang of it pretty quickly. All it takes is a willingness to show up and the humility to learn something new. I'll talk about this more and introduce you to a basic meditation practice you can do at home in Chapter 1 Money Anxiety Disorder. I encourage you to be introspective and take time for reflective sitting—a key component of mindfulness—as we go along. This internal inquiry is vital to shifting your relationship to money and your awareness around your finances.

Reflective Exercises

As you read this book, each chapter will ask you to take some time to reflect and also to journal. You should feel free to do the exercises and meditations in your own time and your own way. You might choose to read an entire chapter, then come back and do the exercises. Or, you might take the chapters linearly, with your journal and pen (or laptop) by your side. There is no right way to proceed with this book. There is only your way. But personally, I love to use a good old-fashioned paper notebook for my journal so that when the mood strikes me, I can draw and doodle as well as write. I urge you to be dynamic and expressive in your writing and drawing and set a goal for journaling for a certain amount of time every day, in addition to completing the exercises in each chapter. Twenty minutes is a good start.

I myself began to keep a money journal when I was eighteen. Along with meditation, it was one of the main catalysts for my financial success and spiritual transformation. There is something so powerful about spontaneously expressing my deep feelings through words, lines, and color. At times I felt so heavy that no amount of meditation helped, and my journal became a refuge, a place to move stuck energy in ways that felt fun. Later, this process allowed me to create solid financial plans and business strategies. I credit my money journal with so many of my financial and spiritual breakthroughs.

One of the purposes of the exercises in this book is to enable you to perceive the internal forces acting on you. Often these forces are not quite conscious, and because of this, they may drive you in directions you don't really want to go. For instance, you may have inherited much of your money anxiety disorder from your family. But, as you become aware of this, it will lose much of its power over you, and you can act more rationally in the present time.

Of course, there are also tangible external forces that act on us, like the ups and downs of the economy and demands in our workplaces or within our families. How you react to these external forces can strongly affect both your happiness and prosperity. As we go along, I'll give you some pointers on how to deal with them. And as you become aware of all these forces and how you react to them, you will become better able to stay more centered and balanced in your life and in your dealings with money. The money anxiety disorder may still be there, but your awareness of it will lessen its impact.

Chapter One

MONEY ANXIETY DISORDER

If you want to conquer the anxiety of life, live in the moment, live in the breath.

—Amit Ray

A 2008 poll by the American Psychological Association showed an alarming trend: 80 percent of those surveyed claimed that the financial crisis was causing them significant stress. This is when psychology professionals first coined the term *money anxiety disorder*. Then *Oprah Magazine* published an article in 2009 and pointed out that women are the majority of the sufferers of this modern affliction.

Money anxiety disorder is the constant worry, nervousness, or unease about money that triggers our natural, habitual survival response of fight/flight/freeze. It's not just a "mental thing," although in a sense, it *is* "all in our heads." Our fight/flight/freeze response comes from a very primal place inside what's known as our reptilian brain: the amygdala. The amygdala is a tiny almond-shaped part of our brain associated with our mental and emotional reactions. It is in charge of when we feel good, euphoric, or blissed out, and it is in charge of when we feel stressed, anxious, and panicked. In a sense, our amygdala is our anxiety control center, constantly alert for danger and ready to set a chain reaction into motion so that we don't get hit by a bus or eaten by a tiger.

In an emergency, our sense organs use their tools—sight, sound, smell, taste, and touch—to send nerve impulses to our amygdala so it can decide instantly whether to institute fight, flight, or freeze. The amygdala then sets in motion a chain reaction of adrenalin and other physiological changes in our body, which prepares us to react. If you've ever been in danger, or thought you were in danger for even a split second, you probably remember the feeling of adrenaline suddenly coursing through your veins. You have your amygdala to thank for that.

The problem arises if we perceive ourselves as being in danger when we're really not. In our stressful world full of pressure and stimulation, our amygdalas are in overdrive most of the time. When the amygdala habitually responds to general anxiety as if there were a real physical danger, the body will eventually become depleted and exhausted. Like an emergency switch stuck on, the amygdala causes our internal alarm system to exist in overdrive most of the time. The stress response of fight/flight/freeze takes a toll on the body, eventually causing somatic discomfort, tightness, and even pain.

But how do we turn the switch off?

How to Tell Normal Stress from Money Anxiety Disorder

Without fear, human survival would be unlikely or perhaps tragically funny. But anxiety differs from true fear. Fear is based on a real event or the threat of a real event—the potential of actual harm to ourselves or the ones we love. Anxiety, on the other hand, is a subjective emotional state that arises out of our thinking. It is not a response to an actual pressing danger, but an elusive reaction to lifelong stress and past experience. Anxiety can cause sweating, increased pulse, shortness of breath, loss of sleep, change in appetite, and other less tangible symptoms.

Of course, we all feel anxiety from time to time. Stress and anxiety are perfectly natural reactions to stressful situations. They alert us to ways in which our lives don't work and allow us to rise and meet life's many challenges. There are a lot of financial situations that call for worry and anxiety: work performance evaluations, losing your job, not knowing if you will be able to pay the rent, buying something you can't afford, not receiving a child support payment you really need. But a normally empowering primal response to problems can become a problem unto itself when it starts to be a reaction to unfounded fears and generalized anxiety.

HERE ARE SOME OF THE WAYS MONEY ANXIETY DISORDER CAN MANIFEST ITSELF IN YOU:

- When you think about money, you feel overwhelmed, panicky, or confused

- You have obsessive thoughts about your or your spouse's job security, income, or spending habits

- You have trouble talking with your partner about money, or money is a primary source of conflict between you and your partner or family members

- When you think about growing older and retiring you become emotional, rather than feeling inspired or secure in your plan

- You experience chronic pain in your back, neck, shoulders, stomach, or elsewhere with no tangible explanation of why

- You often find yourself lying awake in bed at night thinking about money or your future

Just like any relationship, our relationship with money can be a source of great stress and anxiety when not managed skillfully—especially when what fuels our stress and anxiety arises from real or imaginary fear. On the other hand, our relationship with money has the potential to transform our lives and the lives of those around us in rich and abundant ways. When our relationship with money is fear-based, what tends to get carried forward in the world through us in the ways we spend, invest, share, receive, or plan reflects these various unwholesome states, regardless of how much money we actually have.

Stress is our natural way of compensating for the strategies that we have chosen, as well as our body's intuitive way of communicating what is not working. When stress is not managed skillfully and we keep going despite the warning signs, we end up coping with the discomfort of stress by impulsively acting out to relieve the pain. The result is what we too often see in the world: rampant greed, harmful addictions, debilitating aversions, and a tendency to shut down emotionally. Think about your car: ignore the lights on the dashboard for long enough, and your engine will eventually blow up. When we deny or avoid the truth about our stress symptoms, we eventually destroy our own financial life. We can't function with one foot on the brake pedal and one on the gas.

The Two Categories of Fear

The roots of stress and anxiety are often found in two categories of fear.

- The first category of fear is the practical, legitimate fear of not having enough money to save for retirement, pay our bills, or make rent. This is a real fear of not feeling safe and secure, not having shelter, food, and friends, and perhaps of not feeling like we belong in our community and society. All these can be a real source of stress and anxiety.

- The second category of fear is the imaginary fear that we are not safe and secure, even though we actually have plenty of material security. Perhaps this comes from missing an inner sense of safety and security. In this state, we may not feel enough gratitude for what we do have and all the ways that we currently already live in abundance. We fail to recognize that most of our safety and survival needs are already being met. We feel unwarranted stress because of possible unresolved past fears or traumas, which often get projected and turn into a fear of what could happen in the future.

Regardless of the kind of fear that drives us, when it is not held with skillful awareness, understanding, and compas-

Nothing in the affairs of men is worthy of great anxiety.

—*Plato*

sion, the results are a survival-oriented primal response resulting in stress and anxiety. Often we experience painful physical symptoms that come with fear such as constriction in the chest, shortness of breath, a tight jaw or belly, poor digestion, problems sleeping, snappiness, a short fuse, or a tendency to cling to material things. These physical reactions are fueled by all kinds of chemicals released by the brain to help us cope.

Our bodies are designed to mobilize and protect us regardless of our real or imaginary fears. Stress and anxiety are actually the body's protective strategy to get us to respond to our real or perceived threats by motivating us to find a solution. The urge to fight, fly, or freeze is a natural biological survival response—just as it is for animals that face real threats in nature. However, it's often not the best strategy for coping with financial or life-related stress. And when a fear or a survival response orientation becomes our habituated response toward our finances, there will eventually be suffering. We will suffer, our decisions will suffer, and others will suffer.

If we don't take the steps to find clarity and resolution— or a way of relaxing and releasing from our fear-driven past, current, or future financial circumstances—then our financial life will be consistently driven by stress, anxiety, and primal survival responses.

How Does Money Anxiety Disorder Happen? And Why Do We Need a Cure?

The only constant is change. As we attempt to endure the fast pace of our modern lives, money can be a useful tool as a well as a giant trigger around our core survival instinct. Whether you are a boomer, a teenager, a college graduate, a recently released convict, or an elderly retiree; whether you are man or a woman; whether you are young or old, rich or poor, you have probably experienced stress about money at some point in your life. In the workshops I teach, I hear a lot of responses to money anxiety disorder. Things like:

> *"My anxiety about money is off the charts. Every time the first of the month rolls around, I worry that I may not be able to make things work."*

> *"I don't know how I am going to make it on my income."*

> *"I am getting older and can't compete with the younger generation for a job."*

> *"Anxiety about money drives me to make poor, impulse-driven choices."*

> *"My millions are not enough. I need far more than what I have to be happy."*

> *"What am I going to do when I am old and don't have enough money to live on?"*

> *"Sometimes I feel so much anxiety and fear about my financial survival that I would rather die than keep dealing with the unknown."*

We are all vulnerable to anxiety around money and around change. The question is whether this sort of stress pushes us over the edge or inspires us to take positive action.

Personally, I have experienced both ends of the spectrum: spinning out of control with anxiety while trying to keep up with my colleagues and competitors in the real estate industry, and reflecting on my personal prosperity at a spiritual retreat, where I was able to take stock of all the spiritual and material wealth I did have. I am grateful to have been able to make enough money and also grateful— just as importantly—to be able to shift my attitude around my finances so that I now come from a more conscious and embodied place. Of course, I still experience money anxiety disorder from time to time just like everyone else. But I am no longer a prisoner to it. I am grateful to the mindfulness and somatic practices in this book for allowing me to create a more lasting peace in my relationship with money. Now, when I do experience money anxiety, I try to look at it as a messenger who has come to tell me that it's time to slow down and take stock.

The bottom line for all of us is that life can, and at some point will, deal us a different hand than we may have expected. Security is a myth, and we can't control our future. What we can do is learn to re-tool, re-train, and re-align our minds so that we are better equipped—mentally, emotionally, and spiritually—to deal with the fluctuations in our finances and our lives.

Get Comfortable with the Math

For many of us, money anxiety disorder is more like a chronic illness than a curable disease. We might never vanquish it entirely, but we can learn to manage it with the proper "medication" so that our flare-ups are fewer and further between. One of the quickest "no duh" ways to reduce anxiety about money is to learn to manage it better. Although it can be tempting to look for shortcuts or to ignore our finances altogether because the subject seems too painful to cope with, in the end, knowing where you are spending your money and planning for the future are key to financial ease.

Cultivating spiritual tools and a healthy mindset are crucial steps to treating money anxiety disorder, but there is no getting around actually learning to better manage your finances. How much money is coming in? How much is going out? What do you have left over for retirement, savings, and emergencies? At some point, you'll need to become comfortable with these numbers.

Many of us turn a blind eye to our own financials. It's too painful for us to face, and we feel helpful about changing our reality. But not knowing how your own numbers work, or keeping secrets from yourself about your financial reality, is an easy way to self-sabotage. This book is not about how to budget, plan for retirement, or invest better. But as you go down the path of facing your fears about money, I highly recommend simultaneously taking a proactive approach to managing your money. Here are a few practical tips for getting started:

- *Get organized.* A well-organized home office (whatever that space is for you, maybe just a drawer in your desk) is a great way to set an intention around being in charge of your money situation. Take an afternoon to clear out the junk, put things in order and create a proper filing system. Make sure you have places to keep track of receipts, bills, invoices, credit card statements, credit reports, approved loan information, canceled checks, etc.

- ***Create a set time to visit your financial "space."*** Once you have a tidy place for your money paperwork, set a time in your calendar to regularly visit this space and check in. Perhaps it's once a month or once a week. Visit this physical financial area of your life regularly—just like you would visit a garden—and take the time to sit, review, and assess. Treat this space like it's sacred, the monastery of your money.

- ***Create a budget.*** Of all the money management tactics out there, this one is the simplest and also the one most people have the most resistance toward. Do some research and find a budgeting technique that works for you. Having a budget doesn't mean you have to walk around with a little notebook all day keeping track of every penny you spend. And it doesn't mean that you won't get to drink your daily lattes anymore. There is a budget that will work for you. Find it.

- ***Set financial goals.*** Writing things down on paper (or in your computer) is a powerful way to set an intention. What is your vision for your financial future? We'll talk more about goal setting in Chapter 7 Right Intention.

Learning to make positive, tangible change while also recognizing when you have enough is the key to financial and life happiness. We are all familiar with "The Serenity Prayer":

God, grant me the serenity to accept the
things I cannot change,
The courage to change the things I can,
And the wisdom to know the difference.

What "Enough Money" Means

When you have enough money to cover your living expenses and set aside a little bit for a rainy day or an emergency, it is easier to feel relaxed. But that doesn't mean you won't still experience anxiety about things like balancing your checkbook, paying your bills, applying for a home loan, buying a new car, or taking a vacation. And always there is the looming threat of something going wrong: job loss, a break-up, a family member needing a loan. Keeping anxiety in check requires more than just money in the bank. I've worked with people who have more money than most of us could dream of having, yet they still experience anxiety around money. Some of them have fallen victim to their anxiety to the extent that their financial decisions caused an absolute meltdown in their lives. In fact, this mentality is exactly why our country has experienced such catastrophic collective financial meltdown.

Having money in the bank can help calm the survival-oriented anxiety so many of us feel about our finances, but it is not the ultimate answer to money anxiety disorder. In addition to creating a stable financial base, the real answer lies in creating lasting peace and calm internally. The most empowering and effective approach to easing our collective suffering around money anxiety is to start with ourselves. Once we can learn to better manage our own money anxiety, we can be a better example to others. We can become warriors for constructive change. Through inner and outer reflection and inquiry, we can step out of the anxiety vortex and learn to rest and relax around our financial situation. We can learn to respond more skillfully to whatever we face—and this pertains to our finances and beyond. Once anxiety is no longer running the show, we can make wise financial choices around our earning, our spending, our investing, and how we share money.

It all comes down to a choice: what do you want to create from this moment forward?

REFLECTIVE JOURNALING EXERCISE:
How Serious is Your Money Anxiety Disorder?

When you look at your checkbook or pay a bill,
what comes up?

When you compare yourself to someone with money,
what comes up?

When you compare yourself with your neighbor,
what comes up?

When you compare yourself to friends, what comes up?

How does your money anxiety disorder manifest in
your body, your mind, and your life?

Chapter Two

YOUR MONEY STORY

Remembering that I'll be dead soon is the most important tool I've ever encountered to help me make the big choices in life. Because almost everything—all external expectations, all pride, all fear of embarrassment or failure—these things just fall away in the face of death, leaving only what is truly important.

—Steve Jobs

We all have a personal money story that informs our relationship with our finances and how we live our lives. How our parents managed their own relationship with money is quite often how we do it, too. Our dominant story might be "There is never enough" or "I am not enough" or "Money is bad" or "I have to struggle to make it" or "Rich people are evil." All of these storylines, or whatever other personal story you might subconsciously tell yourself about money, arise out of mismanagement of the fears that shape our financial reality.

We All Have a Story Around Money

Both of my parents' senses of financial harmony and balance were hindered by a deep fear and anxiety around safety and survival, but they had very different coping strategies for their money anxiety disorder. My mother had a scarcity mindset and thought if she grabbed and held on to every dollar she would be okay. For my father, money was the root of evil; pushing it away would free him from his pain. The sad reality is that they both blamed money for their suffering, and neither grasping at it nor pushing it away helped either of them find peace.

When I began to investigate my own story around money, I unearthed some old, painful stories I had bought into and was carrying around with me:

- "'Life is a struggle."

- "'Making money is a struggle."

- "'Unless I work hard and struggle, I will never make enough money."

What showed up somatically in my body around these stories in my late twenties and early thirties was a constant struggle to breathe, constriction in my chest, tightness in my shoulders, and a stagnant financial flow. These symptoms of money anxiety disorder often led to even more of a hyper-arousal response, which is a very primal but often over-amplified reaction to real or imaginary survival threats. Habituated responses can paradoxically lead to a downward cycle of stress, anxiety, and self-perpetuated states of pain, suffering, and material and spiritual poverty.

As I started to deconstruct my own stories through years of meditation and therapy, I began to unravel my unique money lineage and saw and held it with compassion rather than impulsively following along with it. I realized these were much bigger stories than I could ever hold: they came from familial and ancestral struggles as well as natural human survival responses. As humans, we've developed responses known as fight/flight/fear based on real threats like being chased by a tiger or dying of famine. The problem is that we have incorporated them into our modern-day imaginary dealings around perceived threats. Of course, there are real threats to our life and livelihood even now. The trick is to differentiate the real threats from the imaginary.

Interestingly enough, our dominant mental money survival story is what we tend to create and express more of in the world in so many interesting and often painful ways, and until this story is met and gently released with compassion and deeper awareness, it keeps us spinning on the wheel of suffering, lack, stress, and anxiety. We've all heard sayings like: "On your deathbed, you won't wish you worked harder." In the end, how important will money be to you and those you love? Weigh the importance of money next to other life qualities like:

- Being loved

- Being generous

- Taking care of yourself

In my mind, the most empowering use of money in one's livelihood is to be an agent of transformation in our lives and

What is your "story" around money?

How much of that comes from your family history?

in the lives of others. Money, after all, is just a tool we use to get those things we need in order to live a comfortable life—in the present and in the future. Money is currency; its intended purpose is for spending, sharing, and investing. Nothing more. Money is like air: it needs to circulate, be breathed in, and be breathed out again. If you take a deep enough breath, can you hoard oxygen? Or let it all out and simply not breathe in again? Not while living! Money is no different. And like oxygen, there is plenty of it to go around. But you can't eat it or build a house with it. It's just one tool.

Speaking of breath, notice your own breath right now. How relaxed are you about letting oxygen in and out fully without worry, struggle, or anxiety? Now imagine this is money you are breathing in and out. How much of it are you willing to let in and release?

Our Collective Cultural Story

In my work, I have interviewed hundreds of people from all walks of life and many socioeconomic backgrounds—rich, middle-class, poor, incarcerated—to get a sense of how each of them defined and experienced prosperity. One of these people was Ben, a UPS employee. Ben was a practical, hard-working American who, despite all the challenges of his life, refused to live from a place of old, painful experiences, and instead, stayed mindful of how his old stories would continually resurface. He made it a practice to show up to work every day, be in service to his job and the public, and manage the little bit of money he had well. He didn't buy into the "more is better" story our culture tries to teach us, but instead lived simply and was happy with what he had. Ben said to me: "I am not greedy, or stuck in my anger and fear; this is the key to my prosperity. I was a Vietnam vet who saw many of my friends die in front of me, recovered from drug addiction to numb out the pain, and now I feel prosperous in that I have a great job with UPS—despite the horrors of having been on the front lines in a war. Now I am practicing showing up and living my life one moment at a time. When I go off into old stories, I hit the gym, call supportive friends, or go fishing. I just can't survive any other way. I love my job at UPS, have managed to pay down my debt, and now own my home free and clear. I just take life one day at a time!"

I love Ben's account because it proves to me that it is possible to free ourselves from our story and our conditions—or, at least, how we perceive our conditions to be. But freeing ourselves from the greater cultural story is another matter. Our culture and the media create a fear-based story that is so tempting to buy into. One day, I decided to scan the headlines to see what the newspapers were reporting on. These are just three of the headlines I came across:

STOCK MARKET PLUNGES BEGIN TO FEED ECONOMIC FEAR

STOCK MARKET TUMBLES AS FEARS OF GLOBAL SLOWDOWN RISES

AS STOCK MARKET PLUMMETS, MOST AMERICANS FEAR NEW ECONOMIC CRISIS

Notice how often the word "fear" is suggested in commentaries about the economy and money. And the stock market, of course, reacts to this collective fear and uncertainty and reacts accordingly. The herd mentality always rules during any national or global financial crisis, and also during a boom, because people are instinctively wired to follow the crowd and accept the group opinion. This is just a natural part of our evolution. We learn exclusively from each other, like a bunch of hyper-social apes. So it's natural to gravitate in the direction the group is moving.

There is nothing wrong with being a part of a social movement that is aligned with our highest intention as a society. The problem comes when markets react to the fear of the people, often hyped up and exaggerated by the media. It is this reaction to real or imaginary fear that leads to a perpetual cycle of fear or greed-based decisions about spending and investing.

When there is collective movement acting out of greed, the market tends to go up. When the collective feeling is greed and loss, the market goes down. Or it is forced to go down to counteract the false up of the previous financial bubble that was created out of greed. Think about our country's recent real estate disaster, which ultimately led to the downfall of our economy. When we buy into the illusion that more is better or that money is bad, we perpetuate this false economy, both as a part of the collective and in our own personal financial lives.

There Is Another Way: The Mindful Way

You see, everything is about belief, whatever we believe rules our existence, rules our life.

—Don Miguel Ruiz

When we are not being aware and present with our current circumstances, then it is easy to get lost and react from our habits or our story: our thoughts, our automatic reactions, the words we choose that reflect our non-present state. Thich Nhat Hanh said: "Every mindful step we make and every mindful breath we take will establish peace in the present moment and prevent war in the future." Joseph Goldstein, a highly respected Buddhist teacher in the West, has this to say: "Mindfulness is the basis for wise action. When we see clearly what is happening in the moment, wisdom can direct our choices and actions, rather than old habits simply playing out our patterns of conditioning."

If we could simply learn to pause and check in about what is really going on underneath the anxiety, fear, and stress of our stories, it would become possible to make more skillful decisions about our money, both on a personal and a collective level. This is where the concept of mindfulness comes in—a technique I have been teaching clients and students for many years. We hear a lot of talk about mindfulness practice these days. But what exactly is it?

Mindfulness is a widely used practice in almost all spiritual paths, but it is called by different names in different traditions. It is discussed in great detail in ancient Hindu, Vedic, and Buddhist texts, and also in the Christian and Jewish faiths, which both talk about meditation. Since introduced here in the West, mindfulness has taken off as the "next big thing" in many spiritual circles. But this valuable practice is not a fad. It's not just something that you do once in a while or even once a day on a cushion, nor is it a state of mind you must attain off in a monastery. It's a useful, day-to-day, moment-to-moment tool that can be used everywhere and in any situation to enhance and bring clarity to our experience and our state of mind.

Even now, as you are sitting and reading, begin to notice your breath. Feel the chair holding you. Notice sensations in your hands, feet, and belly. As you read these words and in-corporate these directions, you are being mindful. When you notice yourself drifting off to follow a thought, but then come back to breathing, you are being mindful. If you start thinking about a bill that needs to be paid, but then you notice this thought, and stay spacious and present with the sensations that come up, without distracting yourself by changing your activity and trying to mask unpleasant sensations, then you are being mindful.

Mindfulness is the practice of simply being aware of what-ever is happening in this present moment. This includes be-ing aware of the stories and thoughts that shape our actions around our finances, as well as unpleasant sensations that arise when we are engaging with our finances or when we are caught in collective societal fear. This idea of a spacious, at-tentive, compassionate quality with our lives and our finances is the practice I encourage you to commit yourself to as a possible path to ease suffering for yourself and others around you. Money has the potential to be an agent of transformation in your life, your community, and the world. It begins with mindfulness. Before I learned the tools of mindfulness, when things were not going well for me financially or personally, I was unable to be present with the painful sensations and emo-tions in my body. By developing a strong mindfulness practice, I began to transcend my own fears and stories around money. Now, I teach these techniques to others.

Being committed to being in the here and now, without the filters of fear and judgment that go along with our usual story—when aligned with wholesome intentions—can lead to greater prosperity and fruitful outcomes. Mindfulness is like a muscle: the more you use it, the stronger it becomes.

How Mindfulness Works

The world and our relationship with our finances can be challenging. However, we can turn our financial world into a place of practice and transformation by allowing ourselves to be more mindful and compassionate. Mindfulness is our innate potential to stay spacious without reacting to what is happening with our finances and to deliberately pay attention to where we are in each moment—to the actual experience, regardless of how pleasant or unpleasant, we are having with our finances and our life—and to feel empowered enough to do something positive about it. It is the key to being alive and engaged with our finances in the present moment. Without mindfulness, it is easy to get lost in the wanderings of our minds, to the fears and reactions to the ever-changing world of our finances, and to material circumstances.

When we can see clearly what is happening in the present moment, our innate wisdom can direct our choices and actions more skillfully, rather than allowing our stories, habits, and conditioning to control us. Mindfulness is like a watchman who protects us from mindless greed and confusion.

Mindfulness provides financial clarity and balance in how we make, spend, save, and share our money. It can serve us in the most humble ways, keeping us connected while paying the bills, asking for a raise, creating a financial plan, or offering or receiving generosity. It allows us healthy boundaries around money and informs how we deal with debt.

When we pay attention with compassion, mindfulness is giving ourselves and others a great gift: that there is a space for our fears, sorrows, gains, and losses all to be held in a peaceful, non-judgmental way. When we are mindful, we are not postponing happiness until something good, ideal, or perfect happens with our financial circumstances. We can experience it now, regardless of how much money we have.

A reporter asked the Dalai Lama, "You have written this book *The Art of Happiness* which was on the best-seller list for two years. Could you please tell me and my readers about the happiest moment of your life?" The Dalai Lama then smiled and said, "I think now!"

Happiness isn't about getting something in the future. Happiness is the capacity to open the heart and eyes and spirit and be where we are and find happiness in the midst of it. Even in a place of difficulty, we can find happiness through compassion for ourselves and others. This type of happiness—true lasting happiness—is different than pleasure, and it's different than the high we get from chasing after something. Warren Buffet is one of the wealthiest people on earth, and he yet he lives in the same house he bought fifty years ago, doesn't carry a cell phone, and has given most of his money away to the Bill Gates Foundation—a charity organization founded by another generous billionaire.

By being present with the sensations that come up in our body, or pausing and taking a breath, or just noting the thoughts that pass through our minds and deciding which ones to follow (or not), we connect to the direct experience of each moment and refuse to take on the burdens of extra baggage from our past or the future. Compassion helps us stay on the path, since no matter how we show up, life can still be very painful. Compassion allows us to be gentle, tender, and kind with ourselves as we stay aware on our financial life journeys.

Mindfulness starts with simply being with your feelings and sensations and learning to listen to your body's somatic responses to fear and the other hindrances that impact your financial and life balance. In the next chapter, we'll talk more about these hindrances.

REFLECTIVE JOURNALING EXERCISE: Explore Your Money Story

What are some of your money stories? How do these stories manifest in the way you handle money? Are these stories true?

What are some of the stories and messages you repeatedly heard growing up? How did these stories play themselves out in your family? When you tune in and feel your body's reaction to the stories, how do you feel? Are these stories true?

What are some bigger collective money stories you hear around you or in the news? How does it feel to tune in to these stories? How are these stories serving you, or not serving you (as well as others and the planet)? Are these stories true?

What can you do to protect yourself from the bigger stories of fear and greed?

What would a more positive message or story be that would better serve you?

How does it feel to shift your focus to a more wholesome message around money? Create a positive message or affirmation such as: "All my financial needs are being met easily and effortlessly." Write this down and put it somewhere so that you will see it every day.

SOMATIC EXERCISE:
Basic Mindfulness Meditation Technique

This is a simple mindfulness meditation exercise that can be
performed anywhere, every day and takes just a few minutes.
While you are working through this chapter, or perhaps for
the rest of the time you are reading this book, or even for the
rest of your life, see if you can take a few minutes every day to
ground down and check in.

Here's how:

*Take a comfortable seat. Feel the support of the earth
underneath you. Take a few breaths. Begin to go inside,
calmly, and explore the following questions, without
judgment or expectation. Reflect and feel in to these
questions and feel free to use your journal to write down
what comes up for you. Just creating a safe space to
observe without an agenda to change anything is often
all that is needed for the story to release and the painful
symptoms to ease.*

Chapter Three

HELD CAPTIVE BY FEAR

Feelings like disappointment, embarrassment, irritation, resentment, anger, jealousy, and fear, instead of being bad news are actually very clear moments that teach us where it is that we're holding back. They teach us to perk up and lean in when we feel we'd rather collapse and back away. They're like messengers that show us, with terrifying clarity, exactly where we're stuck. This very moment is the perfect teacher, and, lucky for us, it's with us wherever we are.

—*Pema Chodron*

Most of our money stories are strongly influenced by beliefs that have been deeply ingrained in our psyches as a result of our childhood circumstances and our cultural conditioning. A lot of these beliefs revolve around fear. Of all the emotions that come up for us around money, fear seems to be the driving condition that is the root cause of most of our issues with money. It's an insidious and pervasive emotion that sometimes disguises itself as anxiety, stress, or irritation. Fear can show up as painful symptoms in the body or in the mind in the form of thoughts and stories that really have nothing to do with our financial reality.

In my years of coaching clients

about issues of money and spirituality, I've witnessed time and again how fear holds a tight grip on our relationship to happiness and prosperity. Fear and money are closely related in our psyches, and when these two things are not managed skillfully, their juxtaposition can lead to strain in all areas of our life and within all of our other relationships. How we meet and relate to fear is our challenge. Often, our fears have nothing to do with the financial realities we are actually facing.

I remember once having a deep, pervasive fear of failing in my real estate business, even though I was considered by most to be very successful. Was there a real threat in my life? No. Nevertheless, the painful physical symptoms that consistently showed up for me around this fear included shortness of breath as well as constriction and tightness in my shoulders, jaw, belly, and back. These symptoms constituted a real biological survival response, but they did not come from a tangible threat. Adding to my pain was my constant scramble to accumulate more and more money in order to feel safer. This—my story around money—was causing me much suffering. Until I was in my mid-thirties and began to do mindfulness work, I was under chronic stress. Ultimately, my liberation from this cycle of fear, stress, and survival-oriented reactions came when I finally learned to relax within myself and trust.

Can you recognize how your own habitual fear-based response to money keeps you confined to a small-minded view of your potential?

The suffering-inducing hindrances of stress and anxiety are often impulsive, unconscious coping strategies that we create and use to numb out around our fears. Our coping strategies are often cleverly disguised as the flashy appearance of success, wealth, excess, overworking, and excessive striving—or forms of escape such as renunciation or collapse. This is where some of the other hindrances come in. When we begin to look at our own money story and which hindrances we lean on, it's important not to judge ourselves. Instead, let's pause, listen, feel, see, hear, and learn from the wisdom and gifts that these "guests" have to share.

Learning To Skillfully Meet and Manage Fear

In my counseling work, I've seen certain people with lots of money act like they are in survival mode and others with next to no money show up in abundant, generous, and kind ways. Just because you have money does not mean you can buy a stress-free life. In fact, the opposite is often true. Our ability to live in a calm state of enough relies more on our ability to cope and trust than it does on what lies in our bank account, although there is something very calming and relaxing when you know you have enough money in the bank. Wouldn't you agree? But how much is enough? I once heard someone say "A rich person is one who knows when he has enough, and can stop accumulating more money." I myself was fortunate to reach this point at the age of thirty-five. I realized that the money I had would be just enough to sustain myself, and so I decided to shift my focus to building up my spiritual bank account. My ultimate goal was to achieve balance. Only you can decide where and how to find that balance in your own life.

Just recently I had dinner with a very wealthy friend who had made her money buying, selling, and managing her properties. She listened to me talk about the Mindfulness & Money workshops I teach, and I could see her interest being sparked. She had no idea what meditation or mindfulness were, but deep down, it was as if her soul wanted to try another way. What I heard over and over from her and could plainly see in her constricted body language was: "I am tired, overwhelmed, scared of being consumed with the time with energy that goes in to managing all of my property, tenants, money, and bills." She had the rare humility to acknowledge the pain she was in as a result of owning and managing twenty to thirty prime pieces of real estate.

When I asked her "If you could start all over, how would you do things differently?" she said, "I would let go, sell, and maybe not even purchase some of my real estate to begin with. Who needs all this stress and craziness? No amount of money is worth this!" She was in a state of overwhelm and collapse because of her fear of being consumed and buried under all the responsibility that comes with having too much. She was caught in the cycle of survival with all her millions and stuck in the illusory fears of lack, loss, and not having enough.

At the other extreme, I recently got a call from a couple who lost literally everything—including their home, money, and financial stability—as a result of the real estate downturn; they now have a real, legitimate fear for their own survival. Even though one friend has plenty of money and the others have little or no money, both suffer from the same symptoms of money anxiety disorder. Both are consumed by the primal biological symptoms of fight/flight/freeze.

Here's a story with a happier ending: A friend who lost all his money in the stock market maintained a mindfulness practice before, during, and after the loss, so his response was "Yes I am sad, angry, and scared, but I am not feeling a need to add mental suffering on top of my existing financial suffering."

Instead, he went about calmly taking action to greatly simplify his life and used his circumstances as an opportunity to learn compassion and acceptance of change and loss—even if that change and loss meant filing bankruptcy at age seventy.

Our Natural Survival Response

It's hard to ignore the fact that we all have inherent, natural biological survival strategies designed to help us avoid and survive real or imaginary danger when it comes to our basic needs: food, shelter, security, and love. Whether our financial life is truly suffering and out of balance or whether we have plenty of money and feel the illusion of poverty, lack, and insecurity, our physiological, mental, and emotional fight/flight/ freeze response kicks in automatically. It becomes easy to slip into a state of overwhelm, desperation, and collapse, which is often followed by the impulse to take unwholesome actions in order to compensate for or soothe the distress signals and symptoms we're experiencing.

If we have inherited a familial dispensation to stress, our nervous system goes into action all too easily to protect us from harm that might actually not exist. The symptoms can show up in the body as subtle signals about what is working and not working for us in our relationship to money. When the lights on the dash have been blinking for a while and a state of overwhelm, panic, and desperation has set in, it is time to recognize and understand the physiological wisdom that is being transmitted through our bodies in the form of sensations. Our body often has a deep innate wisdom to share with us.

If we can't slow down and become aware of the subtle uncomfortable physical sensations of money anxiety disorder (like constriction, aches, and pains compared to the relaxed, soothing sensations of ease and comfort), then we remain trapped in the downward spiral of our story and circumstances and continue to feel victimized. The alternative is to face our financial circumstances head-on from a place of clarity, wisdom, and a balanced heart, with a balanced checkbook also being an ultimate goal.

To navigate skillfully around our financial life requires that we pay attention to our overall fear and stress around lack.

How Fear and Stress Manifest in the Body

Sensations are the sensory motor information that continuously occur in the nervous system and muscle tissue as you engage around your finances: go to work, pay bills, juggle debt. Being able to feel these sensations (as in the expression "listen to your gut") is an important tool in allowing us to direct our attention and focus inward. For example, we can experiment with bringing focus to our chest, throat, heart, back, jaw, and posture and start to simply name the sensations we notice in these various areas: "tightness in my throat," "constriction in my chest," "tingling in my fingertips." When we learn how our body is reacting and responding to information we receive from the outside world, as well as from our own thoughts and perceptions, we begin to be able to separate ourselves from the fear and anxiety we feel about finances.

Often, we have a somatic response to money issues: an actual physiological response to real or imaginary shifts in our financial life circumstances, regardless of whether they are good or bad. And when it comes to money, as with most things, there is good stress and there is bad stress. Good stress can motivate us. It can give us the energy to create, build, and enhance our financial life through appropriate planning and decision-making. It allows us to find our own ideal zone, where we experience balanced effort and energy and where money flows in and out in appropriate rhythm. In this place, we can be engaged and in the flow, but still be vigilant not to overextend and overspend. When we tip over that edge and begin to give too much time and energy without receiving back, we get out of balance. Then we start to experience the good stress again, as a gentle reminder to rein it in.

Good stress is the same kind of stress that athletes experience before, during, and after a race, or that orchestra members feel while playing Beethoven's Symphony No. 6 in front of a huge audience. It's the same stress you might feel when first launching a business that you aren't sure will be successful. It's a low-grade hum, a slight anxiety that keeps you alert and on your toes. Athletes, musicians, and entrepreneurs alike will tell you that this slight anxiety actually helps them perform better. But they will also tell you that they need to be simultaneously relaxed and in the zone to do good work. No doubt you too have been "in the zone" many times. Can you remember those times? It's a great place to draw energy, inspiration, and to do great work.

If we can begin to recognize good stress as the first indicator that we need to make a change, it can become our ally. When the good stress is ignored or blown out of proportion, that's when we start to feel bad stress. When we are overly stressed out, anxious, scared, and caught in the cycle of survival mode, we alert our body's adaptive fight/flight/freeze survival response both in our body and in our brain.

Tapping Into Our Inherent
Mindfulness around Money

When you become aware that you are feeling any of the symptoms of money anxiety disorder, simply stop. Take a breath. Feel your hands, belly, or the checkbook in your hand. Whether you are about to make a purchase or a deposit in your bank account, it's worthwhile to pause and reconnect with yourself first. In this way you can relax and step back from the impulses, stories, and judgments that may not be serving you in a wholesome way.

As we disengage the fear reaction from our story and discern the reality of what is really happening with our finances, we take a first step toward having a more healthy relationship with money. Fear might still be a frequent visitor that comes knocking on our door with good, useful information to share, but as we gain more compassionate awareness about our habituated reactive patterns, our practice is to stay relaxed, open, and spacious so we can make sound decisions and create reasonable limits around earning, investing, spending, managing debt, and contributing to the financial wellbeing of others.

REFLECTIVE JOURNALING EXERCISE:
Exploring Fear

How does fear manifest in your relationship with money?

Is fear a part of your inherent story? If so, how does it get intertwined with your story?

Where and how does fear show up in other areas of your life?

When you encounter fear, where in the body do you feel it? Chest? Heart? Belly? Head?

When fear arises, how is your breathing? Can you breathe into that place until the constricted or painful feeling passes?

When you feel overwhelmed with fear or anxiety, where can you shift your focus to that feels good or brings you joy? It can be in your body, or an activity, or a pleasant memory, or maybe even making a list of things that you are grateful for.

Chapter Four

IMPRISONED BY GREED

Bad habits are like chains that are too light to feel until they are too heavy to carry.

—Warren Buffet

Many of us abide in scarcity mode, never thinking we have enough no matter how much we actually have or need. We worry about money when we are poor, and we worry about money when we are rich. In our minds, we tell ourselves that if we can "just get enough," we will no longer worry. But is that really true? Some of the richest people I've known were some of the most strung out about money.

Greed is a reaction to our fear of scarcity. Greed separates us all into our own little dark, lonely corners. Greed is "excessive or rapacious desire, especially for wealth or possessions." There is nothing wrong with desiring things. The keywords here are "excessive" and "rapacious." When our desire becomes obsession it causes suffering.

I can remember when I first segued from the business world into the spiritual world of studying mindfulness practices. At first, I simply transferred my obsessions and greed from my prior life making money in the real estate world to my new focus on mindfulness meditation. I had thoughts along the lines of "I should be enlightened soon" and "I am the best yogi here" and "no one can accumulate karmic points like I can." I was being just as competitive about meditation as I had always been about capitalism. It took me years of sitting and witnessing this insidious process to finally realize that I was just as greedy for spiritual wealth as I had been for material prosperity. The greed was identical in nature, although it had a façade of holiness.

Greed—whether we're talking about corporate greed, individual greed, national greed, or spiritual greed—goes hand-in-hand with scarcity. It is a reaction that arises out of our fear of not having enough. We cling to what we have, and we grasp for more. But if we could just somehow learn to let our money flow in a healthy, skillful way, we would have a much better chance at getting rid of the choking sensation we often feel about our finances.

A Global Perspective

The reality of the Western marketplace model in our society is that it favors those with capital connections and resources. Our national financial paradigm encourages individual profit, sometimes at the expense of the greater community. This model does not come from a place of malice, but lacks a consistent and compassionate awareness around the three Ps: People, Profit, and Planet. Only when these three Ps are lined up consistently and given equal value can true prosperity be realized on an individual or societal level. The wealth of a community depends not just on money, but also on growth and cultural development.

I teach mindfulness in local jails because I see the fallout that occurs when society emphasizes greed and grasping in all socioeconomic groups. In order to prosper, we must all learn to bring ourselves into a more balanced relationship with one another and with the earth. Without this holistic balance, we have no future, and it doesn't matter how much money we each have saved.

According to a recent United Nations study, the richest 2% of the world's adult population own 50% of the world's assets. The poorest 50% own only 1%. This gap is growing at an accelerated rate. This huge imbalance allows the richest 2% to control not just the majority of assets, but most of the resources, and to manipulate or change the rules, laws, and propaganda through the media to benefit themselves in increasing their share of not just wealth, but eventually water, air, and all of our vital resources. Most of these folks have more money than they know what to do with, and yet they are forgetting the greatest prosperity of all, which would be to end poverty in this world and heal the environment by reallocating resources to help the poor and to build healthy, localized, self-sustainable ecosystems that could create life-serving economies grounded in community values and respectful understanding.

We are all interdependent. We share our natural environment. To live in a way that ignores these basic truths will ultimately impoverish us. What good is your money going to do you if the environment collapses or we have chronic war, famine, and suffering? What if our neighbors resent us because we are hoarding most of the resources, while they are hungry and poor? What kind of life are we going to live and what will we be teaching our children if we don't care for one another and take care of the planet? Our money will be worthless when everything starts falling apart. Just look at all the great civilizations that have collapsed as a result of excess indulgence, greed, and an unsustainable relationship with nature. Look at the Romans, French, Egyptians, Persians, Incas, and many more rich civilizations and wealthy rulers. Could they use their money to hide? No! We are no different. We will all suffer if a shift doesn't come soon. This is just the law of the universe: what goes up must come down.

We are humans, creatures of habit, and even with the siren bells going off, most people are living their lives as if nothing is wrong. I am an optimist, especially because I know what it took my mother and me, and so many immigrants like us, to rise above the economic challenges as well as the constant shutting down of our hearts, minds, and bodies while under severe stress. So I acknowledge the tremendous opportunities we have on this planet. When we are back into our hearts and grounded in our bodies, we can understand, feel, and discover the most loving, sustainable path to our own unique form of prosperity.

Stuck in a Cycle of Suffering

In the classes I teach in the prison system, I work with people who have fallen through the cracks of our society and are in many ways stuck in a cycle of suffering that is extremely stressful. They describe to me that it is often so unbearably painful that they have to numb out from their mental, physical, emotional, and financial pain just to cope. Likewise, many people who are not confined in prisons are also prisoners to their own feelings of pain, fear, greed, and debt. Therefore, I consider the prisoners I work with an amplified microcosm of what many of us are going through in our lives in a way that may seem subtler, but still contains the same devastating effects.

Most of these inmates are victims of abuse and don't have the economic means to get their basic needs met, let alone to start dreaming about what is possible in the future. A lot of them have lost everything, including faith in being able to get back on their feet and survive in a world that they describe as very scary. I share their experience here to point out that human resilience is a powerful thing, and our innate ability to dream, heal, and make a difference, even in the midst of stormy weather, is what makes us human.

During my visits to the jail, I follow the same basic format that I do in my other workshops. After a brief meditation to get the participants to connect with their body, breath, and heart so that they can identify what is real in the moment, I have them feel into and dream about their own unique gifts. What would they like to offer the world if there were no limitations, no risk of failure? Even in the harsh environment of prison, where many of them have hit bottom, the response and joy toward these questions is astounding. Most say, "Well, I have lost everything, and I have nothing else to lose, so why not dream big?"

I have heard female prisoners talk about the possibilities they can imagine. They describe gray clouds lifting, the sun starting to shine, and a joy and pleasure inside that they remember only from their childhoods. When they became adults, they became scared and lost those feelings. In their relaxed, safe state of meditation, they are able to once again imagine a more peaceful state of mind and a sense of community and of being supported and uplifted by one another. They also discover a synergetic realignment with their core essence that knows the way. We all know our way, deep down.

Hopefully, most of you reading this book will never hit bottom to the extent of those I teach in prison, but often, regardless of how much money you have, it is easy to get stuck and feel like a prisoner of your own pain. I think it's enlightening to learn a few things from people who have hit bottom. The wisdom that is still alive underneath their pain and suffering is incredibly deep.

One of my female prisoners expressed that she wanted to work with the elderly because she felt that they are so often ignored and forgotten in our society. Another described how good it would feel to be a fashion designer; the following week she showed the class fifty or so of her new designs. One prisoner wanted to study acting, another open a pet grooming center, and several of the women started talking about forming a partnership when they were released. They shared numerous dreams and had the opportunity to feel joy and to savor the delicious sensations they experienced while brainstorming.

I always remind my students in the jail of how so many great people in history had it just as hard as they do, but rose above the gravity of their circumstances. Oprah Winfrey, getting past severe childhood abuse, realized her dream and gift to the world. Nelson Mandela was locked up for twenty-seven years in a tiny jail cell in Robben Island prison off Capetown. My own mother came to this country with three children, very little money, and no language skills. She eventually became a successful entrepreneur.

Be Mindful of Which Dream You Follow

The big secret in life is that there is no big secret. Whatever your goal, you can get there if you're willing to work.

—Oprah

My sister runs a successful restaurant business that she dreamed up five years ago. She makes ends meet financially, but deep down she loves travel photography. She's had to put this dream aside in order to focus on her moneymaking business. Recently she had an opportunity to expand her restaurant into a chain, but after looking into this possibility, she realized that it was causing her great discomfort and unease to imagine expanding her business this much. She courageously chose not to follow the dream that came from fear. Instead, she followed the one inspired by joy and fun: making time to work less and travel more.

I had a friend who dreamed of living in a mansion, and he made that dream come true. When I saw him recently he was in tears, saying how he had overextended himself financially and was being forced to give the house back to the bank. Another client had once worked for Goldman Sachs and was in so much pain from dealing with making his money from derivatives that he became a drug addict so he could numb out from the stress of working twelve hours every single day. Eventually he was arrested for his nefarious behavior and spent time in prison, which is where I met him. I ran into him in a bookstore recently and am happy to report that he is doing much better. In fact, now he is working in the bookstore, making far less money than he did on Wall Street, but in terms of his personal happiness and well being, he feels immensely more prosperous. It turned out that his personal definition of prosperity didn't necessarily involve a lot of money.

He used the same mindfulness suggestions I'm giving you in this book to reach an understanding with himself about living simply and in integrity.

Hardwired for Fear and Greed

Our grasping for more is often hardwired into our psyches from childhood. We are citizens of a capitalist society living in a world bombarded with messages from the media that we aren't enough unless we strive to be more, have more, and do more. From an early age we are taught to strive for more and better. We learn to be competitive, ambitious, and even greedy. We are taught to hoard and accumulate money, investments, assets, and our things. It's not bad to want stuff or to work hard for money, but there has to be a balance between what we want and what we actually need. It's okay to want a certain degree of stuff beyond our basic human needs. The trick is to find our comfort level, that place that Aristotle referred to as the Golden Mean: where we can live a happy, balanced, productive, and sustainable life, halfway between the extremes of lack and excess.

Money has assumed enormous proportion in American society, but having enough money is a means to an end, not an end in itself. Money is only one component of a happy life; there are a number of other components, many of which you may already have. We talked about this in Chapter 3 Held Captive by Fear when we inventoried our lives.

Personally, in my younger days, I pushed very hard to become wealthy, successful, creative, and socially accepted. Often, at the end of the day, I found myself instead anxious, exhausted, tense, upset, stressed, empty, depressed, and closed off from myself and the world. As the cycle of pushing and striving continued, I noticed my body collapsing. It felt as if my mind, heart, and body were cut off from one another and from any kind of true peace and faith. For many years I operated from this place of deep emptiness. The more I pushed, the more I slid into the darkness that I tried so hard to resist and avoid.

In my mid-twenties I had a chance to make a real estate investment that I was sure would allow me to hit it big and retire so that I could pursue my true passions: art, acting, and other creative endeavors. After spending a year trying to entice, charm, and hustle one Mrs. Johnson, an older woman who lived in San Francisco, to sell her huge, rundown house to me for half the market value, she finally agreed. Someone immediately offered me $800,000 more than I had paid for the property. But I thought, no way; I can easily make $2,000,000 if I rehab and convert it to condos. $800,000 did not sound like enough. Mind you, back in the early '80s, this was a lot of money. But the real estate market was booming, and I had dollar signs in my eyes.

I turned down the offer, broke ground, and began to sink hundreds of thousands of dollars into the project, along with two years of my time and energy. I worked hard and survived on only a few hours of sleep a night. Deep in my heart, a voice was telling me, "This is not a journey to prosperity! It's not supporting you in becoming truly happy and free." In truth, the journey was unpleasant, and my intuition was telling me to bail. I sensed that I was creating more bondage, fear, and greed for myself because my actions were out of alignment with my deeper spiritual values, but I didn't listen because I was blinded by greed, tension, adrenaline, and a huge ego-driven by fear of needing to prove myself so that I would be

seen and loved. More than anything, I was driven by the fear
of failure. I didn't listen to my intuition because I was young,
and I lacked the experience and support I needed from others
who had more experience about timing and real estate cycles.
I was so fixated on the agenda of "making it big" that I forgot
to live with my heart and mind open.

When the real estate market went into a free fall, I was
forced to put all the units in the house on the market and sell
them for less than what I had originally paid Mrs. Johnson. I
managed to pay off my creditors and avoid bankruptcy. But
I was broke. When the real estate market crashed, so did my
dreams of making it big in my twenties. My check for the
proceeds, in the end, was for about $13— roughly fifty cents
a month for all my effort.

I had hit bottom in every way. My situation was dire. I had
close to a hundred thousand dollars in credit card debt and
no savings; I lived in a little apartment; and on top of all this,
I felt bankrupt in many other ways. I had neglected my body.
My love life had suffered. My heart was wounded. Things had
not gone the way I had planned, and somehow my life was
upside down as a result.

Sometimes things have to get so bad that we finally learn
to let go, move on, and find a new way of living or expressing
ourselves. Sometimes circumstances force this upon us. I don't
recommend that we wait till we reach a crisis before we realize
the path we are is not working, but rather tune in along the
way to notice what feels good and what doesn't, and learn to
navigate through life with more peace and ease. I knew along
the way that clinging to my dream of becoming rich fast was
causing me major suffering. But I denied the symptoms and
never really learned how to listen to the sirens. I ignored them,

and I was taught a difficult lesson.

This story does have a happy ending. As a result of my patient and trusting work with mindfulness meditation and somatic practices, I have been inspired to dedicate my life to teaching others the tools that have helped me finally find my own prosperity. My material bank account is bountiful, but more importantly, my spiritual bank account is healthy. I devote most of my time to keeping my spiritual bank account flush and helping others do the same through community service. In my twenties, I would have not imagined this would have even been possible. What made it happen was not a change in my financial fortune or the market, but a change in my own view of how the world operates.

Knowing When to Stop Striving

Through my own growth process, I gradually became aware of the idea that the person who is really wealthy is the one who knows when he has enough. The only way to see this state of things clearly is to operate from a mindful place and learn to abandon one's story and one's automatic fear reaction. It's a humbling and painful process to learn to note when we are reacting from fear, scarcity, and greed. We must apply compassion, awareness, and gratitude in order to combat these suffering-inducing states. We have to learn to separate our wholesome thoughts from our unwholesome thoughts.

Often, people do not know when or how to stop striving. The wealthy keep hoarding and scrambling for more because of a deep belief that if they create an overabundance of money, they will somehow arrive at a state where they are permanently safe from change or loss. Others operate from a state of poverty consciousness, truly believing that they never have enough

> To what extent are you mindful, attentive, and compassionate with your current financial situation? Do you notice how it feels inside when you are not?

and staying stuck in a cycle of living paycheck to paycheck, eternally grasping for the next penny. What a sad story each type has created.

When I began my spiritual journey toward prosperity, I discovered mindfulness meditation. I began to develop a daily practice and go on regular meditation retreats. During this time, my teachers encouraged me constantly to remain mindful, attentive, and compassionate with myself. Slowly, I became more aware of my mind's desperate attempt to hang on and attach itself to the feelings, thoughts, or stories that pass through. I began to see that my response to financial cycles was a habit, and a self-defeating one. Now, as I look back, I can see how much extra suffering my anxious, disturbed mind and body added on top of my real economic challenges.

If you find the time to sit still and reflect, you will see that automatic thoughts pass through your own mind all the time. It is only when we become attached to these thoughts that they become real, triggering physical reactions about the past or future—pain, anger, anxiety—when in reality, nothing is happening except that we are having a thought. In a sense, we create the very reality that our thoughts are fixated on. When this fixation is negative—lack, greed, hatred, aversion, revenge—we can't help but feel bad.

Look around you—with non-judgment and compassion, if possible—and observe what kind of reality people create for themselves or for others when they are investing, spending, and sharing their money from a place of abundance, generosity, and honoring their values versus when they act from a state of fear, greed, anxiety, and lack. How are you choosing to live your life? From a place of love or fear? From an embodied presence or a place of disconnection and anxiety? One leads to more prosperity, and the other to more poverty, regardless of how much money you end up with.

You Are Okay, Right Here, Right Now

When you can relax, breathe, and feel your feet on the ground, you can begin to look around with clear eyes and wake up to the reality of being present with the here and now. You can let go of your projections of future financial ruin. The ability to feel yourself in the here and now will keep you connected to yourself and anchored amidst the fleeting and ever-changing reality of the world in which we live.

By being in acceptance of change and tuning in to any greed, fear, or denial you harbor about money, you can start establishing a more solid ground from which to make sound financial decisions. When you recognize that your number one work in this life is to learn to remain calm and aware in the midst of inevitable change, your perspective makes a dramatic shift for the better. But it can be exceedingly difficult when the change involves your net worth or balance sheet, especially if you have been conditioned to equate money with survival. This paradigm shift is the key to finding true prosperity in your heart. When you attain a place of peace in which to abide, it will support you in making better financial decisions.

Nature provides a great metaphor. Nature responds to change with zero attachment. The mountain doesn't beat itself up when the snow melts or tell itself stories about landslides or hang onto fears about erosion. The tiger doesn't have a story about scarcity when she can't catch the gazelle. She simply tries again and again until she is successful. The redwood tree in the midst of a forest fire can't run, so it stands tall. The same fire that destroys the forest also plays a part in its re-growth. The stream that encounters a rock simply flows around it.

An important aspect of Right Understanding is investing regular time to examine your habits, patterns, and reactions surrounding your finances. It can show you how your relationship to your money might be causing pain and suffering and how it can help you create more prosperity and abundance. Even after all my many years of self-work, I am not exempt from this process. I have to stay ever vigilant and tuned in to my own tendencies around greed. Through the process of being mindful, honest, and compassionate with yourself, you too can gain deeper understanding and awareness around your material circumstances. This will then prepare you to take the next step in creating a plan to navigate through the material world with greater ease, joy, and clarity.

Right Understanding is the first and last step on both your financial and spiritual paths, and it translates to how you choose to live, make money, invest, share, or spend. The mindfulness practice is a tool to explore this way of life.

Shifting from Scarcity Mode to Flow

If we are going to encourage prosperity and abundance in our lives, it is very important to find flow and to shift our focus from what we don't want to what we want and what we already have. In this way, we retrain our minds and develop new habits of seeing the goodness and possibility of what life has to offer us and what we can offer life.

For example, rather than focusing on your lack of money, or your abundant debt, can you focus on how money has flowed in your life so far and how you have saved or invested your money in the past? If you don't have money, can you bring more awareness to potential ways in which you can attract more money? When you earn some money, can you invest a portion of it? It doesn't matter how much money; it's really the intention that matters. When you are able to put aside just a little money every month, you can then pause to notice how it feels to save. As J.P. Morgan said, "There is something calming about having some money saved up." The reasons to save and invest are numerous: for retirement, for college tuition, for emergencies, for a business, to purchase real estate, to be able to help others. Saving is a great habit to get into, because it establishes and confirms your abundant nature, rather than reinforcing fear and lack.

It's important to realize that empowering yourself with savings is not necessarily the same thing as living from a place of greed. Similarly, having debt does not indicate that you live in a place of lack. Not all debt is bad debt. Debt simply means that you owe an amount of money to a person or organization to compensate for funds borrowed. Sometimes, these funds represent capital that you needed to invest in a business—or your life—at a particular time. In the '90s, I borrowed money from a bank to buy buildings in the stagnant San Francisco real estate market. These properties were the foundation of my current material prosperity. I could not be in the position I am in now if I had not been willing to take on some temporary debt. The important thing is that your debt be manageable and impermanent.

Let's be clear about something: banks are in the business of making money by lending money. They are an important and necessary part of our financial system. Banks are not personal. They agree to lend us their money, which really belongs to their depositors, and then we use that money to invest in our futures. Financial institutions often get a bad rap for being greedy, and there is probably something to this opinion. However, my own partnerships with banks have served me well.

I once carried $100,000 in credit card debt, and I didn't want to file bankruptcy, so I had to slowly try to pay it off. Somehow I managed not to miss any payments so I could preserve my great credit rating. But because of this debt, I wasn't able to save any money. Nevertheless, as I paid it down, I felt great because it felt like I was saving. In reality, paying off this debt was just as good as saving, because I was paying off debt that carried an interest rate of 7 to 16%, when the banks only paid 4 to 5% on savings. Thinking about it this way affirmed that I was capable of getting out of debt and finding financial freedom, which I did within five years.

My mom would always remind us, during the minor recessions of the '80s and the '90s, that we are not victims and that we do have a choice about how we respond to our situations. To feel empowered about this process, regardless of the ups, downs, gains, and losses, is very powerful. When we allow ourselves to feel like victims, we create unnecessary suffering. I experienced this firsthand so many times in my life. Even during the real estate collapse of the early '90s, I worked diligently to pay back the bank loans I owed. It was painful, but I knew how important my credit rating would be to me later on if I wanted to bounce back and take advantage of the same lousy real estate market that had done me in. I knew I could make a comeback using a more mindful strategy.

Before I jumped back into investing in real estate, I took

the time to reflect on some of the lessons I had learned in my disastrous prior venture:

- Don't believe everything you read or hear. Take it in, but always listen to your gut instinct first. The media is so often driven by fear and greed, but if you listen carefully, you can discern what feels like valid, useful information.

- There is no way to make a quick dollar. Just as there is no magic way to lose weight,. If someone tells you about a way to make a quick dollar, be suspicious.

- Understand the parallel and also the inverse relationship between greed and fear. To paraphrase Warren Buffet: Be greedy in a good way when others are afraid, and be afraid with a healthy fear when others are greedy.

- Start small. Keep it easy to manage. When I began to reinvest, I bought a bunch of small properties close to each other, with good tenants, in a market that was strong in employment. This was a low-risk venture.

- Most importantly, learn to find authentic peace and joy with your current financial circumstances. Whether you own a home or live in a studio rental, can you be happy with where you are right now and still have goals for the future?

Trying to secure prosperity by making lots of money will

never lead to happiness or a sustained experience of being prosperous, because when we get wrapped up and identified with something outside of ourselves for happiness, we are depending on something that cannot be reliably depended on. Inevitably, we will be disappointed. Whether it's money, a fancy house, beautiful women, a shiny new boyfriend, lots of jewels, or property that we covet and hoard, dependency on anything outside of ourselves for sustained happiness will leave us unstable and insecure, because change is the nature of life. Things are going to change. That is the only thing you can depend on. That means there is nothing outside of ourselves that we can dependably hang on to for a constant and stable experience of prosperity. We will always want far more when we are depending on what we can't depend on. We may not know why we never feel like we have enough no matter how much we have.

The experience of true richness comes from connecting with what you do have rather than trying to find something to fill your void. Interestingly enough, from a place of gratitude and appreciating what we do have, we naturally create and attract more joy, love, and material wealth and abundance into our lives, which, in turn, only adds to our potentially unconditional state of en-joy-ment.

When I retired at the age of thirty-five, I felt like I had enough money. Yet I was not happy or even content. I finally understood that having more money and more stuff wasn't ever going to make me happy as long as I was depending on things outside of my own self. To be lasting, prosperity must be understood as an experience we allow ourselves to have regardless of our material richness. Consequently, no matter how much or little money we have, we can experience abundance.

Collective Greed

When we look at our national and global economy and money culture, it's easy to see how the idea of "flow" is a crucial factor. From a pragmatic point of view, one person's loss is another's gain. In the real estate market, for example, a seller who over-leverages or buys high ends up passing his property along to someone else who was wise enough to patiently wait for the right investment. So from a personal point of view, it makes sense that when times are tough, we should wait it out, and eventually the cycle of flow and abundance will return to us. If we're patient and aware, we learn to recognize an authentic opportunity and act on it.

In the year 2000, there was a lot of hype about home buying, and many people hopped on the real estate bandwagon because of a fear of being left behind. Looking back, we now see that most of the speculative home purchasing happened right at the tail end of the real estate boom. Just like when there is hype around a particular stock and prices bid up, but inevitably come crashing down when the market declines, greed and fear were the biggest drivers in the real estate bubble and subsequent crash. When people are greedy, bubbles get created. When they get scared—or when lenders get scared—crashes happen. This is a collective phenomenon that relies on the base emotions of the masses.

Markets rise, and then they fall. No one is exempt. Many people suffer from this truth. While a lot of folks suffer from financial impermanence, the losses of one person are the gains of another. We are all interconnected. We all participate in this balance. Buddhists call this "non-duality." We are all a part of a greater truth.

On a personal level, however, this phenomenon is not

that comforting. Therefore, in order to protect yourself, it's important to find where you fit in to the greater economic balance of your society and the global economy. When an up cycle ends and things begin to ebb, when values go down and jobs are lost, are you in a position to ride it out? If the market is on the rise but a bubble is being created that will later be inevitably burst, can you sense in your gut that there is something wrong with the big picture?

Personally, I've lived through three recessions, and each time I bought in to the greed and hype that led to the recession and then found myself in an uncomfortable, scary financial position. I overextended myself to buy more real estate and leverage my credit, and I ended up paying for these greedy mistakes. Finally, I learned my lesson and began to apply the tenets of my mindfulness training to my financial decisions.

Time and again I've heard friends buy into the idea that it's silly to work hard or struggle as an entrepreneur when you can simply buy a house and let it work for you. The idea that your home can be turned into a virtual ATM machine to pay for your lifestyle and retirement is absurd in many ways. With deep compassion and empathy I can now see how, in the past, I gave in to the temptations to "get rich quick." But not this time. I finally learned to make my investment decisions from a place of equanimity, clear discernment, and balance—not from greed or fear. Now, when I make a financial choice, I always make sure to stop and listen to my heart and my gut. I also consult my practical checklist: I make sure that I have financial reserves before I invest in something new, and I don't let myself over-leverage. I make sensible investment decisions with appropriate risk that feels comfortable to me.

The Antidote to Greed

The Dalai Lama said that the antidote to greed is contentment. "If you have a strong sense of contentment, it doesn't matter whether you obtain the object or not; either way, you are still content." Also I would add, be content, but don't be so content that you don't challenge yourself. Simply be mindful not to let your journey be run by greed.

For me, the antidote to greed has been a combination of generosity, gratitude, and contentment for what I already have. The only way I know how to balance out my need to crave and grasp for more money is to access my spiritual and creative sides and to be in service so that I can give back, which I do with my Mindfulness & Money courses as well as the work I do in the prison system.

In addition, I've learned to recognize greediness in myself. When I experience it, I don't feel good inside. Perhaps you too can reflect back on a time when you had enough of something, but still reached out and grabbed for more. Maybe you took a few too many cookies at a Christmas party; or perhaps you packed your schedule with too many activities. Maybe you heard about a too-good-to-be-true investment and jumped on it without doing proper due diligence. These can all be considered lessons learned, as we become better and better at noticing hindrances that come along to thwart our prosperity.

SOMATIC EXERCISE: Assess Your Level of Financial Flow vs. Constriction

Let's take a deep breath and take a look at your finances. Open your checkbook or log in to your bank online and see where your money is going. Look at your savings, your retirement account, and your most recent paycheck. Take a few deep breaths, relax, and drop into your financial life in a deeper way. Check in with your body.

Where do you feel the money energy flowing?

Where do you feel constriction?

Where do things feel stagnant?

Where do you feel most generous, open, and spacious?

Pause, breathe in and out, and let go of what you have just learned. Be in this place of nonattachment to your money. Enjoy the inflow and the outflow. How does it feel in your heart and body?

REFLECTING JOURNALING EXERCISE: Reactions

What tends to be your reaction when money flows abundantly? When it doesn't? Here are some questions to ponder and journal. It's a good idea to complete this exercise on the heels of the meditation exercise above. That way, your answers will come from a calm, centered place within.

Do you make money decisions from a place of clear awareness or from some unconscious habit or pattern?

Do you notice a difference in the outcome when making decisions from either a conscious or unconscious place?

What is your understanding of why, as a collective, our society has suffered so much during this recession, and what is your part in this cycle?

What is your understanding of how you can end the cycle of suffering with your own finances?

What will you do now to create more balance in your life? How will you live more fully in the present moment? How will you practice more generosity?

Chapter Five

BEING AT PEACE WITH WHAT IS

Know thyself.

—*Ancient Greek aphorism*

If I had to sum up one goal I have for me and each of my students and readers, it's to achieve balance of both our material and spiritual bank accounts. Without both, we are in danger of bankruptcy. It's sort of like sitting on a chair with a broken leg. We can probably pull it off for a while, but it will be quite wobbly and awkward to stay balanced for the long term. If we take the time to repair the leg, from that secure foundation we can rest comfortably and feel supported.

Even though most of us want the same things in life and may be at different levels of development around health, happiness, comfort, and money, how we each go about responding to real or perceived financial challenges and uncertainty will be totally different. There is no right or wrong way, just your way that feels balanced.

Regardless of how uncertain, turbulent, and challenging your life may be, there are plenty of opportunities and places to pause, breathe, and reflect on your material and spiritual states as well as on your conscious or unconscious coping strategies, and to be in the warm home of your body and heart as you willingly explore your finances and your relationship to money. This type of refuge is available to you all of the time and helps support the cultivation of deep wisdom, courage, and resolve so you can continue showing up with compassion and joy and tend to the garden of your financial life.

The ongoing tending of your spiritual garden will result in the kind of prosperity that is both quantifiable in terms of financial balance and will offer results in the form of joy, pleasure, and positive sense experience that sustains you emotionally over time. It is the foundation of everything else. So it's best not to shortchange yourself at this critical stage of development. If, along the way, you forget to be mindful about your current state, then simply bring yourself back. No worries. You can always pause, breathe, notice yourself getting caught up in your story, notice heavy emotions that spiral out of control, and take a moment to come back. Feel sensations in your belly and chest. Feel how your feet ground you into the earth. Feel the freedom in your hands. Tap into the places—the sensations, sounds, smells, and images—that support your joy and nourish you. Every time you pause and check in like this, you add to your prosperity account.

Staying in the Here and Now

In my own experience, when I am doing something mundane around my finances like paying bills or balancing my checkbook, my mind can so easily get away from me. I find myself complaining, experiencing lack and constriction, bringing on tension and stress and sometimes even a full anxiety attack with survival symptoms: blood rushes to my head, my breathing becomes shallow, my belly tightens. It's as if I am about to be attacked by a tiger! When I fail to pause and regroup, it causes me great suffering. But with experience, I am now able to pause as soon as these stories and symptoms arise. I come back to feeling what it's like to slow down and be present. I simply feel the checkbook in my hands, the pen I'm holding, the slow process of writing out the check, and the gratitude I can feel for those who provide me with water, power, food, and my other material needs—all of which I pay for with money. When I pay my mortgage, I honor the partnership I've formed with the bank, which is a reciprocal arrangement. It is so easy to complain about banks, especially in this current climate, but I remind myself that banks serve an important function in my life and in our society.

Similarly, when I receive a payment from a tenant whose property I own, I take a moment to pause and feel the love and generosity inherent in their check. This type of appreciation is something I cultivate in a long meditation retreat. But I get it just as surely during the quick, daily practice in my real life. It is available to me all the time.

When you can learn how to rest in this warm and supportive place, you can feel free and alive, regardless of what shows up in your financial life. You can respond from the "here and now" intention of meeting life and your finances head on and allow the mystery and magic of life do its thing. This skillful cultivation of wisdom and faith allows us to trust that we will be safely held by the world. The good news is that this can also be a fun process. Life is already serious enough. But like any creative or spiritual practice, once you establish your groove, you'll witness the bounty of abundance. When the need arises and there is a rainy day in your life, you will have created reserves to draw from.

Moving On from the Past While Staying Grounded in the Present

Every day is a journey, and the journey itself is home.

—*Matsuo Basho*

When you live your life and make your decisions based on your old stories, memories, and habits, you stay tied down, spinning and overwhelmed. Ultimately your goal should be to stay alert and vigilant but still relaxed and honestly able to assess the state of your spiritual and material bank accounts without fear, always making sure they feel tended to in a way that feels abundant but not neurotic. When we live our life from the past, we make constant withdrawals from our spiritual bank account in the form of resentment, fear, shame, jealousy, greed, and confusion. These things just lead to more suffering and eventual spiritual bankruptcy.

This is not to say that it's okay to focus so entirely on your spiritual happiness that you don't stay grounded in a pragmatic reality about your material life. I recently spoke to a friend who, at the age of seventy, can no longer afford the payments on his home. For many years he has spoken to me of how his spiritual bank account was overflowing with great friends and abundant happiness. But he has simultaneously displayed a level of anxiety about his diminishing savings account, because, as an artist, he has been unwilling or unable to upgrade his work to meet his costs. He has long insisted to me that his spiritual bank account would pay his mortgage. Well, it hasn't. Now, he is facing the possibility of being homeless. The good news is that his spiritual bank account is intact, and if he can manage to reconcile the practical reality of his finances with his inner world, he will be fine.

I often sail in the San Francisco Bay. Before leaving the dock, I always conduct a thorough run-through of the boat's mechanical and navigational system, the weather and tide conditions, and the communications mechanisms. I check in with each crewmember to ensure that we will have a fun, safe journey. There are plenty of times when the wind gusts far exceed my expectations and I begin to feel overwhelmed, but by staying calm and telling myself to breathe and stay connected in my body, I am able to also stay viscerally connected to the boat, the crew, the wind, and the water so that I can navigate and steer in the direction I want to go. There have been times when I've been stressed and could not communicate skillfully, and as a result the boat has gone off course. Our finances react in much the same way. When we navigate through the world of money, we have to stay calm and grounded and present.

Staying engaged and present with what is up for us around our finances and taking skillful action that keeps us on course toward our desired destination can be a thrilling ride with many great benefits. Or the ride can be a source of suffering or even disaster. At the end of the day, what matters the most is not how much money you have, nor how spiritual you are, but how you relate to your life and the amount of joy and peace you are able to cultivate on your journey. Most of the students who attend my workshops are experiencing some kind of turbulence in their financial lives. I love teaching the Mindfulness & Money course because it helps me remember how to cope better with ongoing change. It's a way of staying sober, in some sense, from the addiction to fear, old useless stories, anxiety, and unconscious ways of coping with the pain such as overeating, drinking, overworking, or collapsing into denial.

One Student's Experience

Start by doing what's necessary; then do what's possible; and suddenly you are doing the impossible.

– Francis of Assisi

I once had a student named Simon who had signed up for an 8-week Mindfulness & Money course I was offering. He signed up for the class thinking it would be mostly about making more money. He had just lost his wife in a tragic accident, and understandably he was carrying not just the grief of the loss and having to raise a daughter alone, but he was also struggling to make ends meet. He was a contractor, and business was so slow that he could barely pay the bills, so he started playing the stock market with the little money he had in reserve. He was basically gambling and looking for a quick solution to his deteriorating financial situation. He was overwhelmed by fear of not making it, fear of the unknown, and fear of not feeling financially secure. He, like so many of my students, came to me thinking that I could offer him a shortcut to making money and managing his financial issues. He was looking for someone to rescue him. When I explained that I could not offer a quick solution, his initial reaction was frustration. I assured him that by practicing mindful, compassionate awareness around finding a comfortable place within himself to rest and be at peace, then he could approach his finances from a relaxed, clear mind and body grounded in the here and now.

Simon decided to try it. At first, he was anxious, scared,

and edgy and just wanted to take care of his immediate survival needs. His body posture, how he held himself, and the tone of his voice reflected the survival-oriented state in which he lived. But after a few weeks, he began to get the hang of the somatic mindfulness exercises we were doing. He began to get in touch with actually feeling the difficult sensations he was having in his body. He began to open up to his grief, sadness, and pain—both around his wife's death and in regard to money. He began to display a kind of relaxed, integrated mind, body, and heart presence in class. As the weeks unfolded, he noticed that his new approach to his financial situation came less from a place of scrambling and desperation and more from a place of ease, trust, and an expanded capacity to meet himself and his circumstances with more compassion and clarity. He realized, as so many others do, that his willingness to start where he was would be the journey that would lead him to financial and spiritual balance.

As a teacher, all I did for Simon was invite and guide him back to himself. I did not fix or enable him, but simply empowered him to learn to draw from his connection to his innate inner wisdom. Doing this alone is powerful, but doing it in a group setting and being witnessed by others seems to bring about a deeper shift. So often, we are too busy to pause and connect with each other. By seeing how others are benefiting from the mindfulness practice, the participants in my groups hold each other up. By learning to reconnect with the here and now, they are actually supporting their own parasympathetic nervous systems in a way that brings about calm and ease, as opposed to the fight/flight/freeze reactions of the parasympathetic nervous system, which cause us to latch onto desperate survival strategies such as robbing a bank.

When Simon regained his grounded, calm core, his more aligned presence affected the entire class in a positive way. There was synergistic movement away from fear and toward skillful action. They became teachers for each other. This is what I encourage in my classes. We are the change, and with every shift, others can benefit. By exploring our ideas, fears, and worries around money in a community setting, we are able to work through our feelings of shame and isolation and realize how much we all have in common. What Simon does with his financial situation and how he manages his stress going forward are up to him, but I have now offered him some powerful tools to use on his financial journey.

Revisiting Your Story

I decided to start anew, to strip away what I had been taught.

—*Georgia O'Keeffe*

As you begin to learn to be a compassionate witness to your internal weather in the present moment, I'm going to ask you to go back in time to the early part of your story. What was your family's general money mood? The general mood of my family, for example, was a lot of fear, anxiety, and struggle. As immigrants in a strange land without much money, we were in survival mode most of the time. Even after we had our basic survival needs met, we were still always in fear of losing our safety and security.

What was true of your family? Was there enough money to be comfortable? Apart from money, was your family generally content? Happy? Or did you experience a lot of anxiety and discontent? How did your parents manage their own external and internal weather?

Even a family without much money can be generally content. By contrast, a wealthy family might be quite dysfunctional and unhappy. Take a little time to sort out the emotions and messages you experienced as a child about happiness and contentment as well as money. What we experienced as children is often what we struggle with as adults, too. My parent always fought about money, and so I grew up with a lot of conflicting messages: it's good, it's bad, it's hard to get, can't trust anyone around it, don't have too much, don't have too little, etc. Each of these messages has its own unique weather pattern (bright, sunny, hurricane-force winds, tornadoes) and its own unique landscape (tropical, desert, fast-flowing river, deep ocean), so finding a skillful way to navigate it toward a balanced spiritual and financial life is the ultimate test. Learning to navigate my own story was my greatest gift to myself, and with empathy I can now understand how others get caught in the turbulent sea of pain and uncertainty surrounding money.

It is so easy to confuse having money with happiness. I certainly did in my early years. In America, in particular, we are conditioned to believe that more money automatically leads to more happiness. The fact that there are some very sad millionaires and some very happy low-income people often gets lost in the face of this dominant belief system.

The first step in your financial journey is simply to come home to yourself. It is urgent that you begin right now, because our time on this planet is limited. Along the way, you will meet many diverse and interesting teachers who will show up to offer you reflections, suggestions, and obstacles to overcome. Your money is one of those teachers. It can be a real catalyst for positive change. Think of it not as a resource to hoard or squander, but as a tool that works best when spent, invested, and shared.

How Mindfulness and Money Relate

I am not a financial advisor or planner, but, given the amount of time I have spent understanding and exploring both of these paths—and my personal experience of when, where, why, and how money flows in my own life—I have gained much insight into the merging of mindfulness and money. When I am in a state of fear and constriction, my relationship with money gets stuck.

I had lunch with an old real estate colleague of mine who felt called to engage in creative projects, but felt constricted about how to free up his time and responsibilities. He complained that his real estate holdings were generating a ton of cash, but his inability to find balance was having a huge impact on him physically. He was tired, stressed, and drinking away his money anxiety disorder after work each day. When we talked about his dream of taking a sailing trip to the Caribbean, he lit up. But he felt constrained by the obligations and commitments he had created for himself professionally. After we talked for a while, my friend realized that even taking just a few minutes to drop into the fantasy of being the captain of his own ship—imagining that he could delegate his real estate responsibilities in order to go off on a sea adventure—provided a useful shift from doubt and fear to joy and peace. Similarly, in my work with prisoners, giving them the tools to pause and remember their dreams, experiences of happiness, and hope for the future can provide a way for the lights to come on. The key is to keep the lights on by constantly making an effort to remember gratitude and the triggers for one's own personal joy.

Like my real estate colleague, I, too, once felt so imprisoned by my financial ambitions and the money construct I had established for myself that I could not imagine another life. Thankfully, I was able to escape my spiritual bondage and find another way. I did this by learning to pause and listen to my heart whenever the opportunity arose for me to make a choice. Now, when I am confronted with symptoms of money anxiety disorder, I take the time to pause, do a quick body scan, breathe, and re-center myself. This way, I can better navigate through whatever financial circumstances are facing me. If you can learn to give yourself and your finances the time and compassionate space to explore and investigate what is up, this simple act of being present will lead to new insight and, hopefully, clarity. In the midst of financial chaos, when I took the time and space to sit in front of my books and check in with my body, something certainly shifted. It was the beginning of a new relationship with money; it became a catalyst for awakening and opening my mind and heart to the new financial and spiritual reality I want to create—one based on trust, balance, and flow.

Integrating awareness around the body and mind with your checkbook may not lead to instant success, but when combined with support from a skilled and reputable financial planner, accountant, or other type of financial consultant who is aligned with your intentions, goals, and values, the results can only be positive. The key is to build alliances with those who will support you in building your financial house and simultaneously feel into your gut-level sense of the people and organizations that you work with. Ask yourself: How does it feel to seek help from this person? Do you feel a "yes" in your head, heart, and belly? This is the balanced approach! If you get a "no" on any level, it may be time to pause.

Ultimately, it will be you who has to decide the course of your journey, and as we have seen in the last recession, giving our power away to the so-called "experts" can be a disastrous mistake. The tools and stories I mention in this book will support you to draw from your innate somatic and intuitive wisdom.

Wherever you are in your journey, right now is the perfect time and place to begin exploring and reflecting on the state of your spiritual and material bank accounts. Yes, there will be twists and turns on the path ahead of you. But each moment can be an opportunity to cultivate greater awareness around how we can show up in relating to our finances with greater clarity, compassion, and balanced effort. Money then becomes just one more catalyst for transformation, regardless of the details of your financial circumstances.

SOMATIC EXERCISE: Assessing Where You Are

Let's take a moment to figure out where you are in your journey and your present relationship with money. We'll begin in the way that I start many of my classes.

Sit with your eyes closed for a minute or two, and ask yourself what your "internal weather" is like at this very moment. What is going well in your life? What are the things that bring you happiness and satisfaction? Feel what gratitude is like in your body. What are the felt sensations? Can you remember these sensations and these thoughts? If so, you can come back to them on a regular basis when you need comfort, safety, holding, and reassurance. This is a natural place to rest.

Continue to sit. Just as the weather changes, allow dark clouds to roll in with the form of negative thoughts. What are you anxious and fearful about? What painful story continues to surface? Take as long as you need until the truth comes to you.

Now, without reacting from a place of habitual impulse, try to stay with the uncomfortable sensations, feelings, and thoughts with spacious, compassionate awareness. Notice any constriction in the chest, tightness in the jaw, shortness of breath, anxiety in your belly, worry, sadness, doubt, or grief.

The point of this exercise is to expand our capacity to be all that arises and passes away, and not allow our nervous system to fall into an automatic, reactive survival mode.

After years of practice, I have discovered that the more I can be open, curious, and comfortable with my internal weather patterns—including moods, stress, and sensations triggered by fear—the more I am able to handle the external changes in my financial circumstances, as well as societal economic changes and shifts. The commitment to this process of being vigilant and aware is like developing a muscle.

Be gentle and have fun with this process. If at any time you feel that being present with what is arising becomes too intense, it's okay to get up and go for a walk, take a break and do something else that brings you some comfort and peace. But always keep coming back!

REFLECTIVE JOURNALING EXERCISE:
Where Are You At Right Now?

Inquire within about the following questions. It may be helpful for you to journal your thoughts and answers to these questions now, in the beginning, and then revisit them when you are finished with this book. See how your answers and reflections might change.

What, if any, aspects of your life are you sacrificing in order to make money?

Do you live in denial about money? Is there an element of avoidance in your relationship with money when paying bills, balancing your checkbook, or dealing with debt?

How do these patterns affect your health, relationships, or your ability to live fully in the "here and now"?

Imagine you knew your life would end six months from now. How would you live your life differently in the here and now? What kind of relationship with money would you create now?

What if you had five years?

What will you do now to create more balance in your life? How will you live more fully in the present moment? How will you practice more generosity?

Chapter Six

IMPERMANENCE

That nothing is static or fixed, that all is fleeting and impermanent, is the first mark of existence. It is the ordinary state of affairs. Everything is in process. Everything—every tree, every blade of grass, all the animals, insects, human beings, buildings, the animate and the inanimate— is always changing, moment to moment.

—Pema Chodron

We borrow everything we have for a relatively short period of time. Even our bodies go back to the earth. Hopefully, we use what we borrow not just to make ourselves content and prosperous, but to share what we have for the benefit of others. This goes for love, for friendship, and for money. Learning to let go of attachments is one of the core teachings of the Buddha, and it works just as well in our financial life as it does in our spiritual life. All we can do is be the best caretakers we can be for what we have: our money, children, homes, possessions, body, wisdom, ideas.

Form is impermanent. Another way of saying this is, "If you're born, you will die." We may not always want to admit it, because we don't want to lose what we love. But in our hearts we know this is true. Reactions to this knowledge differ depending on our habitual way of being in the world. One person may be scared, greedy, trying to hold onto everything they have and accumulate more and more. No matter how good their bank balance is, they always see financial ruin around the next bend, like my grandfather. Another might try to beat change by running even faster, working every minute. Yet another is reckless: if fortune is not going to last anyway, why not spend it while we have it?

For many people, perhaps most people in the United States, our economic wellbeing is synonymous with survival. When we have "enough" wealth, whatever that may be for us, we feel secure. So when we come face to face with the impermanence of our economic state—when the bottom drops out of the market or we suddenly win millions in the lottery—this can literally create panic. Panic triggers a surge of adrenaline, the automatic fight/flight/freeze response that is inherent in our biological makeup. If we are in real imminent danger, this is a great response that can save our lives. But if the mind exaggerates today's minor market fluctuations into something much larger and more threatening tomorrow or reacts to a real financial crisis by sending the body into a chaotic reaction, this response can throw everything out of balance.

This is just how it is in this world. Even with the best of intentions, there will be loss and gain, fame, and disrepute. Buddha calls this the ten thousand joys and the ten thousand sorrows that we all face on this planet. The good times may fade, but tough times won't last. Soon you will be able to get back up and continue building your assets, investments, and bank account. You know the saying, "The harder you fall, the higher you bounce!"

It seems like magic, but it's really how life works. Get

clear and connected with your intentions, calling, and passion, then apply balanced effort held with patience, and a passionate ease and surrender to the outcome, and before you know it you are creating both material and spiritual wealth. The universe we live in is benevolent and caring, despite the curve balls it throws at us on a regular basis to make sure we are paying attention.

The Truth of Impermanence

I'm sure you are familiar with the saying "Change is the only constant." Impermanence is a fundamental law that applies to everything. Indeed, it applies to money in terms of our personal finances, the stock market, the real estate market and debt—both our own and our collective nation's.

Being aware, in acceptance and at peace with the nature of change and uncertainty is the key to true prosperity. Mindfulness techniques can help us achieve this peace. At this point in this book, my hope is that you have developed some good tools to use in your own quest for peace, balance, and prosperity.

Using the ups and downs of the world of money and finances as a path to spiritual liberation may sound strange, but this is the path that I have chosen to gain deeper insights that have liberated me on so many levels. I've spent many years contemplating the parallels between my spiritual life and my financial life, and here are some of the similarities that I have come up with. Perhaps you will relate.

1. SEEING AND RELATING TO IMPERMANENCE

It's fairly obvious how the concept of impermanence applies to our financial lives: money comes and goes—sometimes more, sometimes less, and with varying speeds and velocity. Sometimes the source, like a well, may dry up for any number of reasons including job loss, bad investment decisions, or how you choose to spend, share, or invest your money. Or maybe the source dries up because of the choices and behaviors of others who you trust to invest your money for you. Just look at how thousands of people were affected by the Bernie Madoff Ponzi scheme in the early 2000s.

The flow of money rises and falls— just like the seasons, the weather, and our own emotions, thoughts, and even our breath. Dividends rise and fall. Even the real estate I own is constantly fluctuating in value. Just like my body, money is falling apart constantly and has to be kept together through ongoing maintenance.

Eventually, it will all fall apart or disappear. This is the nature of life! And as long as you are clinging and grasping to keep it from changing or claiming more than you need, or pushing it away, you will constantly be adding more pain and suffering. There is a fine balance, as we discussed in the last chapter, between clinging and letting go. Of course, you need to preserve money in order to invest in your future and put it to work for you. As long as you can utilize your available financial resources with skillful, sustainable, and caring means, you are on the right path. It's possible to plan ahead and have goals, to be reasonable and practical with money, and even to dream big without being so attached to your figures that you will fall apart if they vanish.

Just like your material bank account, your spiritual bank account is subject to change. Your moods, feelings, and thoughts will fluctuate and sometimes seem unbearable to manage. Every time you become aware and present with change and relax around it, you make a deposit into your spiritual bank account. This account can be developed to the extent that you are committed to showing up and being compassionate and present with the way things are in this moment. If we can let go of our resistance, our stories, and our reflexive grasping and aversion around gain, loss, sickness, old age, and death, we can learn to face change with equanimity.

I recently had a conversation with my teenage daughter about the impermanence of the comfortable world she lives in, where she is used to a nice house, car, and plenty of money when she needs it. I want her to grow up with a real perspective on the reality of this world. So we did a visualization exercise around what it would be like to wake up hungry or lose our home like so many thousands of families do every day. We then visualized what it would be like to live through a famine, a war, or any of the other experiences that humans regularly endure all around this world. This may seem like a strange way to spend quality time with my daughter, but I was proud that she could not only grasp the importance of the exercise, but also drop into the visceral connection to the reality of how things can change at any moment for any of us. The idea of this visualization was not to scare her, but to teach her comfort in the midst of the potential for change.

2. ABIDING CALMLY IN THE NATURE OF CHANGE

By direct observation and through focused awareness around change, we can observe the nature of how things are indeed always changing and not spin out when big, abrupt, painful changes occur, even out of left field. Learning to abide calmly in the nature of things starts with the basics: noticing the breath coming and going, hearing the sounds around us, then taking it a step further: looking at our check book or our credit card statement, as we did in the exercise at the end of Chapter 3 Held Captive by Fear. That exercise is a great way to gauge the extent of change happening in your own financial life. Noticing how your money life changes regularly—the amount coming in and the amount paid out—is a great practice to gain insight into the nature of impermanence. It helps train us to regulate our nervous system so that when there is change, we don't react from our habitual fight/flight/freeze instincts.

Sometimes we hang on to a view or story about our finances and cling to how we think things should be instead of being present with the actual reality of what is going on. In the hundreds of interviews I've conducted about prosperity, I notice two predominant and extreme views:

"I need more money to feel safe or okay about myself." Often the reality is that there is plenty of money and what really needs to be looked at is our fears surrounding our ideas of safety or worthiness. We may have an attachment to more money when we are actually attached to the idea of what money will bring us or do for us.

"I don't need money to be happy, and I can just be spiritual and creative, and it will all work out." The attachment to this view is often a source of suffering because it's hard not to stress when there is not enough money coming in to pay the rent and bills.

3. FINDING SOLACE IN FLOW

When you are mindful and aware of the ebbing and flowing nature of your finances and can learn to skillfully manage and engage in this flow, then there is a good chance that you can make financial decisions from a clear, discerning place and not from a habituated survival-oriented place. Mindfulness can be a great way to be with the show of life as it unfolds, even through the scary scenes.

Being Willing to Let Go

In Zen Buddhist practice it is often said that the span of our lives is like a dewdrop on a leaf: beautiful, precious, and extremely short-lived. Life is remarkably unpredictable. Whatever you want to accomplish, whatever is important to you, do it and do it now—with as much grace, intensity, and sense of ease as you can muster. None of us knows what life will bring. In any moment everything we take for granted can change. We must be careful not to dwell on impermanence constantly to the point that we become paralyzed with fear of loss, but we can use an awareness of change on a deep and wise level to focus our priorities and increase our appreciation of the sheer beauty of existence.

Mindfulness helps us to see that our ideas about who we think we are can be limited and inaccurate. What we mean when we say "me" and "I" are often incomplete in profound ways because the reality is you can't take ownership of anything that is subject to change. You can benefit from the many gifts money offers you, but to build an identity around it, or around debt, or around lack and scarcity, is not very skillful and will lead to suffering. Ultimately, you have to be willing to let it all go.

"Your self worth doesn't equal your net worth," as they say, so don't let your self-identity fluctuate as your financial circumstances change. If your happiness is tied to your net worth, high or low, or to the stock market, then a good practice for you is to learn to stop and connect with that which is stable and consistent right in the here and now: change, breath, sounds, earth, faith, community of friends and family, your god, and your meditation practice. What else can you connect with that will support you to be at peace and at home in your heart and body?

Everything is constantly changing: cells, individuals, communities, nations, the planet, and even the Milky Way. We have to be skillful and discerning about how we show up for it all. What is the most skillful way for you to be in balance and learn to let go? This is a very personal question, and no one else can tell you the right answer. For me, it was learning to let go of greed and recognize that it causes suffering. What do you need to do to find your own unique balance?

When winter comes, the bear goes into her cave to hibernate. She comes out again when things warm up, well rested and ready for the hunt. Sometimes our personal (and the national and global) financial cycles call us to go inward, to slow down and rest, and to wait for the next upswing. At other times, you have to take action: wipe the slate clean and release whatever is not working in your life—a job you are unhappy with, investments that aren't performing well or are misaligned with your core values, friends who aren't supportive and caring. We do the same sort of thing when we prune away the dead, diseased, and damaged limbs of a tree, allowing new growth to begin.

Here's the bottom line: the changes in the financial or real estate markets may not always be predictable, but you can be certain that they will change. Change is inevitable! This understanding—that impermanence is the natural state of everything on earth—is an important key to maintaining your balance as you negotiate the waves of changing economies. However, it's important not to let yourself fall asleep at the wheel when change approaches. The good news is that all things pass—even the tough times. Markets decline, bottom out, and rise again. When we feel stretched financially, if we can persevere, stay focused and diligent, and stick to a sound business plan, we will always eventually get out of the slump.

Cultivating Skillful Means

We can't evolve if we don't take some kind of risk. We must risk failure, love, approval, and desire. And things may not work out in the way we plan or fantasize. We may have the best of intentions and choose and embrace a plan, or go forward with a great project, and yet there is always still a risk. My own real estate development project is a good example. Even at times when I thought the risk was minimal and the market conditions perfect, there was always still a risk that the market could change and the risk increase. And it did. In our financial lives, there are so many variables. Just when we think we have enough money, a project falls through or an unexpected bill shows up or there is a natural disaster that derails us. Hurricanes and earthquakes and tsunamis and fires come unexpectedly and destroy lives and millions of dollars worth of property on a regular basis around the world. None of this is personal.

Even here in America, the land of freedom and liberty, people are subject to these things and others—like the risk of drug addiction and unhealthy lifestyle choices. On any given day, you could be diagnosed with cancer, get run over by a drunk driver, or be a victim of a drive-by shooting. There are risks inherent in just being alive, let alone all the other risks that we have to take in our dealings with work and money. The heart of prosperity sees this, somehow embraces it, and in some ways even moves toward it. This way, we face our fears directly and recognize through practice that what makes life exciting, interesting, and worth living is the many unknowns and risks.

We must always be prepared for the changes that come with each passing cycle. All aspects of impermanence can be transformative. They can all lead to deep prosperity if we are centered and balanced. The world gives us many tools with which to better prepare ourselves. The Buddha calls this "cultivating skillful means." Using skillful means to approach your financial life will ultimately benefit all parts of your life. Here are some things to keep in mind:

- **Don't lose faith.** Things will eventually change for the better. Keep moving forward, even if it means you have to start over from scratch. Imagine the worst that might happen and sit with this image until it no longer frightens you.

- **Stay calm as you plan your financial future.** Take regular breaks to breathe and collect your thoughts to ground and center yourself. Feel the earth solid under your feet.

- **Invest time getting to know people in your community.** Especially if you plan on asking them for favors. People are less guarded and more willing to help and support you when they feel your sincerity. Explore to what extent you are open and generous, how it feels, and what it looks like. Explore to what extent you are not open and generous, and how it feels, and what it looks like.

- **Invest in expanding your knowledge and wisdom not just around the subject of money, but around yourself.** It's the highest form of investment you can make in yourself.

- **Retreat.** Enjoy the harvest of the good investment decisions you made during the slow times. Slow down and fill up your spiritual bank account. As you start saving and investing, manage your money wisely; keep it running optimally so you can take advantage of the inevitable downturn. This is a mindfulness practice in itself. Instead of the focus being on the breath and thoughts coming and going, you can practice being with the flow of your finances and choose to make wise decisions that have a wholesome financial outcome.

- **Be generous.** Especially if you tend to hold onto money! Give time, energy, support, and money to those in need. Remember to maintain compassionate boundaries! Being generous does not mean rescuing others, as this may actually prevent them from learning how to make it in the world.

- **Be a lighthouse.** Allow your love, kindness, wisdom, clarity, and compassion to flow out of you freely so others will become inspired.

- **Flow.** When you encounter a rock in the stream, flow around it. Remember the lessons of nature and use them.

SOMATIC EXERCISE: Sitting with Change

This is a simple, practical meditation practice to understand and skillfully meet change as it arises and passes. Start by sitting in an upright position in a comfortable chair. Feel gravity anchoring you, and begin to bring awareness to the ways change is presenting itself to you even now. Set a timer, if you'd like, and spend about two to three minutes on each of the following aspects of your mindfulness experience.

BREATH: notice your breath coming in and out. The breath is such a powerful reminder of change and so symbolic of how money comes and goes as well. It's also a great way to come back home to what connects us to a very essential life force.

THOUGHTS: As you sit still, notice how thoughts come and go. You can't stop them even if you wanted to. I once heard a teacher say that in a thirty-minute meditation session, some 350 thoughts or so pass through one's mind. Trying to control or stop your thoughts would be like trying to control the wind or the climate. Instead, simply notice as they come and go.

SOUND: Listen carefully and notice how sounds around you rise and fall, and how each sound is unique compared to the next one.

BODY SENSATION: Notice both pleasant and unpleasant sensations in your body. Not all change is comfortable to be with.

OPEN UP TO EVERYTHING: Sit and open up to everything that arises and passes away; sound, thoughts, feelings, and sensations. Develop a container to hold it all. If it becomes too much, go back to one area of focus. The breath is a good home base since it's happening all the time and is so life-giving.

MINDFULNESS EXERCISE:
Notice the Nature of Impermanence

Now that you have had some experience with the basics of mindfulness meditation, begin to apply what you have learned to your relationship with money out in the world. Open up a financial magazine or newspaper or turn on the financial channel and notice that everything, from the stock market to investors' moods and reactions, is constantly changing, as is the media reaction and coverage. What thoughts come up for you around all this?

Chapter Seven

RIGHT INTENTION

The key to a good life is finding the balance: time for painting, time for friends and family, time for teaching and giving back, time for contributing to the community. I find that this balance is always changing; it is not the same from year to year.

—Stephen Quiller, famous artist and teacher

The next time you get a chance to watch Wall Street traders in action, notice their body language. They often look constricted, tense, and shut down to an exaggerated extent. Their facial expressions, their hunched shoulders, and their tone of voice are all indicators of extreme money anxiety disorder.

I remember Alex, a former Goldman Sachs trader who took my spirituality class in one of the jails where I lead mindfulness groups. I had the pleasure of teaching him how to meditate and be more accepting and relaxed with his emotional and physical pain. Like so many Wall Street traders, he had once looked successful on the surface. Before imprisonment, he had been rolling in cash and flash, but somehow never felt satisfied with his material success or comfortable in his own skin. Because he did nothing to ever replenish his spiritual bank account, he short-circuited the process of spiritual balance by constantly using drugs, sex, and gambling as ways to cope with his fears. Eventually, these habits spun out of control and he ended up behind bars.

After months of quietly participating in my spirituality classes while serving time, Alex began to open up about his deepest fears. One of the main reasons that I like to teach in jails is because I can relate. I went through a similar process to Alex of feeling unworthy, alone, scared, and greedy and then acting out and numbing out. I know the feeling of looking in control while actually being internally out of control. Lucky for me, I did not end up in jail. There, but for the grace of God, go I. Through my work in the jail system I have met many inmates who, just like everyone else, want to be happy and experience love, security, and peace in their lives. Unlike some of us, they have taken wrong turns along the way or lost touch with their moral compasses. This is not as hard to do as we might think.

For Alex meditation provided a support so he could learn to "come back home" to himself and get in touch with his deeper discomforts. His fear and anxiety about money had led to his impulsive need to act out with drugs, sex, and over-working. Alex began to realize that what he really wanted was to be able to accept himself exactly as he was and to live a simpler, but spiritually richer life. Once he learned to sit still through the initial discomfort, he discovered he could open up to the sensations that were buried underneath the surface and deal with the difficult emotions and thoughts that occur just because we are human. He realized that no matter how much he had tried to escape his real or illusive pain and fears through drugs, sex, money, and material worth, in order to be truly free, he had to sit still without any distraction. Unfortunately for Alex, like so many of those in complete denial, finding this answer meant first hitting complete bottom with financial and spiritual bankruptcy.

This story has a happy ending. When he was released, Alex traded his job at Goldman Sachs for a simple but spiritually fulfilling job at a local business. He loves his new job and his new life and has been able to cultivate a more wholesome relationship with money. Alex is a success story.

Get off the Boat Before It Sinks

Hopefully, you are not yet and never will be on a sinking ship, either financially or spiritually. But perhaps you notice leaks in your financial boat or in your life in general. Now is the time to take action and turn this boat around. If you notice destructive behavior in yourself, it's time to take action and change it. If you know that you tend to overspend or go further and further into debt or that you don't value your time and your worth in regard to work, it is time to do go into proactive repair mode before you end up in a complete financial shipwreck. If your boat has already sunk, congratulations! There is only one way to go from rock bottom.

The practice is the same for all of us. Once we have learned the basic tools of mindfulness, we can pull them out at any time and apply them to transactions and behavior about money. The extent of your commitment and your attentive focus and clear presence around your finances allows your body's innate wisdom to provide gut-level guidance. The extent to which you can maintain loving compassion and, perhaps, forgiveness toward your financial shortcomings will lead to inexhaustible amounts of prosperity because there is no gift more precious than being present with life in the here and now.

As an immigrant, buying into the "more is better" motto of the American culture cut me off from the essence of flow around how I managed my finances and my life. Refusing to be skillful about navigating through all the pain and uncertainty I was creating just led to more pain and suffering. It was basically a domino effect. Living from a state of ego-inflated, fear-based reaction turned me into a shark who only attracted other sharks to my shark pool. We were all on the prowl for blood, and it was every shark for himself. In the fight/flight/freeze model, I was a fighter. Maybe you freeze or flee instead of fighting. It doesn't matter; the outcome is the same.

When you're suffering from money anxiety disorder, adrenaline can be very addictive. It's no coincidence that Alex, the Wall Street trader, with his adrenaline-seeking addictive personality, was drawn to trading on the stock market floor as well as sexual addiction and compulsive drug use. Finding a community that could support and nurture his spiritual needs from behind bars was his saving grace.

I have the honor, through my work with prisoners, of witnessing their transformation as a result of the hard work they do while serving time. Once during a group discussion on money and mindfulness, I listened while an African-American crack dealer named Jerome told the group: "I should have followed my dreams and become a basketball player. Instead, I chose to deal drugs and was making a thousand bucks a day. I was able to buy my kids everything they wanted for a while. But now I am here, and I wish I had followed my dreams in sports." I'm guessing that Jerome was probably very focused and present during everything he did in his life prior to jail, whether it was playing basketball or dealing drugs. But his intentions were unwholesome. Imagine what he could have accomplished if his focus was placed on a more constructive path?

When Jerome finished speaking, a middle-aged man in the group spoke up. "We can't feel sorry for ourselves, but we can make a shift. We chose our paths, and now we have to pay. You were a crack dealer on the streets? Well, I transported tons of drugs from the Caribbean to Miami. I was making $20,000 a day. I also had kids and a wife. This was my livelihood, and even though it supported a grand lifestyle for my family, it wasn't sustainable. And now I am paying the price, and my entire family has to suffer as a result. You will be out of here in a year or two. I will be here for many years. So stop being a victim; get out there and create the life you want!"

I was scared that a fight might break out between these two men. But instead, Jerome began to weep, and so did a few other men in the group. Jerome said, "You're right. I want to choose another path. I am tired of looking for shortcuts and easy money." The group, as a whole, nodded their heads.

This is a segment of society that has gotten caught up in wrong livelihood. However, let's not kid ourselves. There are many people out in the world committing the same types of crimes as these prisoners who will never get caught, particularly white-collar financiers. But just because they don't literally end up in prison does not mean they are not living in a prison of their own design. Prison looks different for each person. Being imprisoned by your own greed, fear, and grasping around money is just as painful as being in an actual jail. It can be harder to get out of this sort of prison.

Imprisoned by Greed

In my younger days, my financial intentions were deeply rooted in fear and greed. The fruits of my unwholesome intentions were reflected in lots of debt, financial loss, and poor health. A lot of bad karma can be created when your intentions are not wholesome. These days my financial reality reflects a more appropriate intention of generosity and mindfulness around money. As the saying goes, what you sow, you shall reap. The extent of your prosperity will often be a result of the extent of how skillful you are in navigating through your life, especially around your communication skills, your ability to set intentions and goals, the way you handle stress and anxiety, and how skillful you are at earning, managing, investing, spending, and sharing your money.

When we are not conscious and instead react from fear, greed, and unskillful action and speech, we create poverty and suffering on many levels. Right Intention is the foundation that supports everything else that you create in your life. Everything rests on the tip of intention. I can say from experience that when my intention is consciously or unconsciously rooted in the hindrances, then what I create more of in life often reflects this way of being. It extends and is expressed in the work I do, the way I spend, invest, or share money, and in the relationships I tend to create. It results in distorted thinking that affects my action.

Clarity of intention is critical if you want to be supported by those who are motivated by love and joy and other such heart-based attributes. If you lose your clarity and focus or can't find your center, be prepared to meet a barrage of temptations from every direction that will try to convince you to shift your values toward greed, fear, and consumption. But these indulgences only dull and numb the mind and heart, not to mention that they have the potential to wreak havoc and create financial ruin. The practice of holding your boundaries with kindness and firmness of heart will serve you well at all times, but especially in times when you are vulnerable. It is an invaluable tool to know when and how to say "No!" or "Enough!" or "Stop!"—both to ourselves and to others.

FOR INSTANCE, COMING FROM A PLACE OF...
Results in such distorted thinking as...

...FEAR
"I have to protect myself and my stuff from getting hurt or from loss."

...GREED
"There is never enough, and I better hurry and get as much as I can, any way I can."

...DELUSION
"I have no clue and feel helpless and hopeless around my finances; I just want to crawl into my shell. If I pray or meditate enough money may fall from the sky."

... AVERSION
"Money is the problem. I just can't stand it any more. The top 5% are bad; the bottom 95% are lazy."

What distorted ways of thinking throw you off balance? Do you have a tendency to slip into greed, delusion, or aversion? How does it feel? How do you re-group or come back to balance? Since I have a tendency to be thrown off balance by slipping into greed, I balance it out by doing a consistent gratitude and generosity practice. Just feeling into what I have a lot of and how I can be of service seems to be my personal remedy for greed. What is it for you?

The ability to keep your balance is the key to negotiating impermanence. The cycles of life and money are inevitable, but you do not have to fall off with every turn of the wheel. If you do, how do you get back on track? Can you have fun and be playful with this? I can almost say that it is a given that I will be slipping on and off the path, but I seem to get back on quicker as long as I can laugh at myself: "Ah, there I go again! Wow, this is what it's like to slip into fear, greed, or reactivity. Let me now just get back on the path. Here is the breath; here is the sensation in my belly, hands, and feet; this is how my heart feels. I can love, accept, and forgive myself just the way I am."

It is challenging to maintain balance even when we are doing a good job managing our financial responsibilities. But when we avoid them, let debts pile up, or deny the fact that there is more money going out than coming in, we eventually lose our balance and fall. The real skill is to be able to step back calmly, look at the situation dispassionately, and discover which adjustments are called for in this moment.

Goals That Come from Clear Intentions

In the course of teaching Mindfulness & Money classes, I have interviewed hundreds of people suffering from money anxiety disorder including quite a few wealthy people and several real estate tycoons, as well as a number of artists, those struggling to pay rent, and even homeless people. With each person I spoke to, regardless of the amount of their personal wealth, I wanted to know their intention behind their wish to be prosperous and successful.

One interview was with Jim, who participated in a partnership that owned millions of square feet of office and retail space. Jim made it clear that his entire success rested on Right Intention. In fact, before he opened up to me he wanted to know if my intentions were aligned with his. After some talking and sharing, he felt the resonance and agreed to share his views on Right Intention. Here is what he told me about his keys to success:

- Be very clear about what you want and where you want to go.

- Find resonance with your vision in the people you work with.

- Don't chase after things—markets, real estate, or people. Instead, be patient and allow things to come naturally to you.

- Don't be attached to having to have something. Be able to walk away and let the deal go.

- Stay in your heart and work only with people who share a vision of an economic win-win model. This model must be based on the intention of mutual understanding and aligned with deep values.

Because Jim's goals rested on clear intentions, he had created an extremely successful business. Jim's story points out the necessity of clarifying the intentions that underlie your goals. When goals arise from heart-based intentions and a deeper commitment to align the mind, heart, and body, only goodness can arise. When you commit to enlarging your world to include more people, you enlarge your spirit.

Definitions of prosperity are as unique and diverse as there are people. The journey of prosperity is not just about achieving a final outcome or getting the things that make us happy, but rather the way we engage, interact, and relate to ourselves and others while on the journey. True wealth comes about as a result of right effort, action, speech, intention, and mindfulness.

Throughout this book, my intention is to offer you questions, ideas, and suggestions about how to cultivate the skills necessary to come into greater alignment and resonance with a deeper, more authentic prosperity that is unique to you—not just based on your traditional money story or your cultural story and conditioning, but from a more embodied, soulful understanding that is generous, kind, clear, and balanced. It is through living skillfully with mindful awareness and compassion that you can achieve unlimited prosperity: money, wholesome relationships, good health, and the ability to respond to life's many challenges by turning them into opportunities for transformation.

Skillful Intentions

What is the authentic source of what you really want in your financial life? Once you can pinpoint this information, you can begin to create a moment-by-moment, day-to-day, week-by-week action plan to inspire you, mobilize you, connect you to your goals, and help you fulfill your intentions around money and your life. In order to get there, you need to learn to stay consistently present and embodied and always have compassion for yourself, no matter what happens.

My intention for a long time was not very heart-centered, but instead came from a disconnection, confusion, and a false perception of what true prosperity was. My intention came from a place of fear and greed. I thought I needed more money to feel good and worthy of love. As a result, I suffered quite a bit, because both my financial and spiritual accounts were built on the foundation of confusion. Only later, as I learned the skills to be more embodied and aware of the importance of a solid intention grounded in the soil of my heart, was I able to build a financial reality that reflected ease and clarity. It became clear that what I wanted to share was support for others who also want positive change and prosperity, but like the old version of me are confused and stuck. I chose to teach in the jail system because on some level I could relate and feel empathy with prisoners in their reality of being "trapped." In the Mindfulness & Money courses I lead outside of the jails, I focus on building awareness of how to find financial and spiritual freedom. My student base ranges from crack dealers to prostitutes to white collar criminals to folks just hanging on to their jobs and trying to pay next month's rent. The principles of mindful, attentive awareness around intentions, goals, and action steps are universal and apply to all of my students.

I love using my mom as an example because she is a strong and capable woman who has always known what she wanted in life. She has always been willing to share her intentions, goals, budgets, skillful action, and unwavering moral standards. Her intention from early on was to become financially successful so that she could help other single mothers and those in need. As a kid it was easy to rebel and not understand this, but eventually I remembered what she had shared with us growing up. Through diligent work and unwavering focus she managed to create a stable financial life and a sense of security for herself and her future as a single woman. There are thousands of self-made women and many who are minorities and single mothers like my own mom. If my mom, who started as a Persian immigrant with nothing in a new country, can succeed, I am confident that anyone can.

My mom said to me: "First, you must decide what you want; then, go for it. If you get thrown off track, get up and go again. But always do it with integrity and sincerity. Then, people will naturally want to do business with you. You must remember to save your money, invest it, don't waste, be frugal but generous, travel and see the world, pray a lot, and never lose faith." Wise words that I carry with me to this day.

To reach her goals around material wealth, she put in the time and energy for many years. She got up at five every morning and was out the door by seven, back home at noon to make her kids lunch and prepare dinner (and maybe take a little power nap), then back to her real estate office in the evening. During the day she would knock on dozens of doors, and, in her broken English, offer her real estate services. In the early days her car was so beat up that her clients had to get in from the driver's side. She was humble, and she persevered, and she is still enjoying her real estate business to this day. Even in the beginning, she reaped the benefits of her hard work and commitment to her clients: on the weekends there were non-stop parties at our house with musicians, dancers, and families all coming over to celebrate life together.

When your intention is to create or share love, creativity, and abundance, then what often follows is more of the same.

This is how our universe works. There is no judgment or blame, just something to reflect on and observe in your life. If your intention originates and is held and sustained from the soil of the heart—a deeper, more compassionate awareness, generosity and loving kindness—then the fruits that thrive from your prosperity garden will be abundant and will reflect your wholesome, skillful intention.

Intention is the first step, but goals are also crucial in getting you to where you want to go.

Goals

Goals help you create your place in the world and be an effective person by enabling you to take certain steps to move forward toward your desired destination, whether that be achieving a certain income, a retirement goal, or in my own case, enough cash flow to sustain the kind of lifestyle I had chosen and to free up my time so I could give back to my community. Remember that being grounded in intention is what provides integrity and unity in your life. Through the skillful cultivation of intention, you learn to create wise goals and then work hard toward achieving them without getting caught in the attachment to the outcome. Your intentions become the guiding light on your journey.

Goal setting is an important component of financial balance and stability. Goals are action-oriented, concrete things that help us carry our intention, vision, and ideas forward toward actual effort and quantifiable results. Creating wholesome, clear goals is critical to achieving success. Starting with skillful intention is the way we connect and align our heart, mind, body, and checkbooks with our highest values. Clear goals are then set to actually help you move forward toward a desired outcome and are supported by action, effort, and skillful communication.

Once we've established Right Intention we take the next step, which is to set goals based on those intentions. Then, we create a structure in our day-to-day lives that allows us to meet these goals. From intention through goal setting and then by way of structure, we create success and prosperity.

Here is an example of a general intention: "To have a liberated, comfortable relationship with money and to give back to my community."

This sounds great and is probably the intention of most of us. However, in order to get there, you must create specific, measurable, result-oriented goals.

Let's turn that intention into a concrete goal: "By this time next year, I will make enough money working thirty-five hours a week that I can volunteer at a local organization for five hours a week."

The next step is to come up with a few related actions and practices to get you going on your path to achieving your goal. For example:

- I will keep track of my spending for one month.

- I will create a budget and figure out exactly how much money I need every month.

- I will figure out how much money I need to make per hour in order to work only thirty-five hours a week. I will make a specific plan each month for things I can do professionally to increase my income.

- I will take ten minutes a day to sit quietly and notice what feelings, thoughts, and sensations arise and fall away around my finances.

- I will research local volunteer opportunities and reach out to the ones that seem like a good fit.

Now, sometimes things are just out of our control. Goals exist to give us milestones and parameters, not to make us feel guilty if we don't succeed. It's crucial to be able to apply compassion and forgiveness to yourself and the process. To stay on track with your finances you have to tend to your finances just the same way you tend to your breath in meditation practice: when you get off track, you simply come back. If you slip in your resolve to save money, or not spend, or focus on any of your other financial goals, you keep coming back to your original intention, just like you come back to the breath. Use concentration and resilience as tools to acknowledge how money is just another type of energy that supports and sustains you. You can make "tending to your day-to-day finances" a soothing ritual.

Finding Support

The other piece of the financial mindfulness practice is to create a consistent accountability and support structure for your journey. This might include budgeting, debt management, or other supported plans. Like I mentioned above, this might mean assembling a team of consultants to help you with your financial planning. These consultants might range from an actual financial planner to your accountant to your CPA (especially if you own a small business) to support groups like the Mindfulness & Money courses that I lead. Other options for support include a Mastermind group, a personal coach, or even just a friend who is willing to check in with you regularly and keep you accountable to your goals. Building a community around you that supports your financial and spiritual goals is like having a church or prayer hall in which to reflect and meditate and make a collective shift.

In the groups I facilitate, I am able to keep others and myself accountable while we together cultivate more skillful habits about money and a deeper awareness of ourselves. What I've found is that being able to accept this kind of support takes a lot of humility, because often what gets exposed is that we are all only human and vulnerable. We all make mistakes and fall off the path here and there. We all face the same human conditions like loss, confusion, greed, and delusion. Having a person or a group of people you make commitments to continuously reminds you of the power of being present and compassionate with the way things are.

In one recent sitting group I facilitated in a local jail, I had the privilege of observing how the mindful support of a group of peers can be incredibly uplifting even for those in troubled circumstances. We sat in a circle and each woman took a turn naming an intention they wanted to manifest in their life. One said that she wanted to "better manage stress," another to "learn to forgive myself," yet another to "stop manipulating people with my speech." We started with a general theme of "What is suffering? How are we responsible for our own suffering?" From here, I was humbled and honored to see how these women owned up to attitudes and behaviors that had not served them in the past and made a pledge to work on themselves with the support of their peers.

A support system can also remind you not to take yourself too seriously. In our prison sitting groups we keep a focus on fun and play—shifting away from heavier feelings like hopelessness and resentment and toward a more lighthearted, accepting view of life. Time and again I've found that a playful physical embodiment of the present moment can help to vanquish feelings of isolation and despair. But when those feelings creep back in, the practice is to pause, re-center, and check in with your heart, body, and breath. A support group can help remind of this practice, again and again and again.

Right Livelihood

When we talk about creating intention, structure, and systems in order to better deal with money and our lives, the first thing we tend to look at is how we actually make our money. In other words, what do we do for a living? Our personal and collective financial security and stability depends on the values that are reflected in the daily work we do, as well as the extent of our alignment of our economic activities with shared values.

At its most basic, our goal is to make a fair, livable amount of money in exchange for our work and talents, to invest in a way that is socially responsible, and to spend our money on goods and services that represent our values. If we could all do this successfully, imagine what kind of a planet we would live on. Imagine our level of true prosperity if we could fill up both of our bank accounts—the spiritual and the material. One is quantifiable with numbers and the other one is hard to quantify but vital to our wellbeing and our very existence. In my opinion, finding the balance between the worldly and the spiritual is the ultimate prosperity goal. Like the Buddha, I recognize that material possessions will not make me

What do you hang your dreams on? What are your values? What is your calling in life? How are your values and calling aligned or not aligned with your overall intention?

happy. But unlike the Buddha I have to live and interact in this world, so I can't just avoid the idea of money altogether. Again, it's about finding balance.

As I listen to the folks I cross paths with every day in my teaching, I hear such common themes as:

- "I want to do a job that makes a difference, but also pays me enough to get by without struggling."

- "Being able to afford health care, college costs, and an occasional trip somewhere fun is what matters to me—plus have more free time to be with family and explore my creativity."

- "I am tired of this system; I am tired period; I can't make it any more."

- "It's all their fault that we are in this mess: the rich people, the Republicans, the Democrats, the bankers, the lenders, the landlords."

Earning, saving, investing, and spending money in ways where everyone wins means living with our deepest values and respect for ourselves, one another, and the planet. I call this sustainable prosperity because, put very simply, it is when success, profit, gains, and advancements occur because of our intentions, goals, and efforts—not at someone else's expense.

It is life affirming rather than life destroying. In this age of global warming and the constant potential for environmental disaster, as well as the huge disparity between the haves and have-nots, our wellbeing, the wellbeing of others and the planet's wellbeing have to be taken into consideration with every decision we make if we are going to survive. Sustainable prosperity is about making choices in our lives that don't cause harm to anyone, period.

Ask yourself if the work you do can be truly said not to cause harm to yourself or anyone else? When looking at how your work impacts yourself, think about how it impacts your health, happiness, and wellbeing. Are you willing to take a stand for the most supportive, safe, and healthy environment in your workplace?

When you engage in work that you enjoy, that increases your wellbeing, and when you choose work in which you can express your wisdom and creativity for the benefit of all, you are engaging in right livelihood. It is a win-win model that does not cause harm on any level and is a one of the ways of making our lives richer and the planet a better place.

There are many spiritual and economic traditions in which leaders have come up with rules and lists to attain right livelihood. Here are my suggestions based on my spiritual studies as well as my practical experience with students I coach:

- Do not engage in work that is stressful, harmful, or toxic, either physically or mentally.

- Avoid work that is exploitive in any way of you, the customers, the competitors, or the environment.

- Be paid a fair living wage in exchange for what you are offering.

- If your involvement and participation in this work leads to huge profits or an increase in income for the company, there should be a fair and equitable distribution of the profit to everyone, not just the shareholders or the CEO of the company.

Of course, these are ideals. Your reality might be very different. If it is, I'm not asking you to make a violent change or to judge yourself harshly. Instead, take a look at where your reality is out of alignment with your ideal and start to notice places you can make small, reasonable changes. The truth is you might not fully enjoy your work, and it may not entirely fulfill you, but this job might be a bridge to get you somewhere else and eventually help you fulfill your own creative expression. Rather than getting caught up in adding extra pain and suffering around your current work, see if you can have a different kind of relationship with it. See the value of how the work may serve as a bridge so that you can eventually make enough money or gain enough experience with a certain skill for as long as it is necessary.

It is important to keep in mind that our middle class ideals are tied to having a decent job, earning enough to pay the bills, and—more now than ever—having some money left over for a rainy day. Sadly, our confidence has eroded quite a bit over the last few years. Incomes are not rising, but the cost of living is. Jobs are harder to find, and it's becoming more and more difficult to stay faithful to our ideals.

The good news is that the economy is constantly shifting. In fact, one recent shift holds a lot of promise: the green economy. This sector could restore a rapidly disintegrating American middle class, not to mention add a whole new way of measuring prosperity and productivity which includes good health, vibrant communities, and a healthier environment. These are awesome markers of prosperity.

Investing in Your Life

Your job is just one way to make money. Taking wise, calculated investment risks with your money is another way. You can work for money, and you also can invest your money so you can have more money later in your life. Many people are happy living paycheck to paycheck. I personally would have trouble living this way, because I savor the option of taking some time off if I need to and don't want my income to stop if I do. So this means an arrangement has to be made so that even if I stop working—either as a choice or as a necessity—my money will keep working for me.

Saving and investing money (even small amounts) will help you to create more financial flexibility and stability in your life. Begin by exploring how much money you would like to invest. Then look at the variety of investment vehicles that you can choose from and their levels of risk and return. There are real estate, stocks, bonds, mutual funds, CD's, peer-to-peer lending, precious metals, and commodities. There are plenty of resources that can help you get started with investing. A money manager or financial advisor can help you make detailed decisions about how to invest your money.

My personal passion has always been in income property. I love the hands-on aspect of being able to go to a physical property that I own in order to get a sense of things. I can touch it, see it, and interact with it. I also love real estate because of the huge potential for passive income, equity growth, tax benefits, and the possibility of leveraging a small amount of money to buy and control many properties in partnership with banks. However, every investment market goes through ebbs and flows, and the real estate market is no exception to this. If you don't learn to roll with the ebbs and flows and develop a savvy investing sense, you can put your time and money in jeopardy. I have been through many ups and downs in the real estate market, and it's taken me a while to come to a place of knowing how to time the market so that I am not buying at the peak and selling at the bottom when things are rough.

Regardless of the investment vehicle you choose, it takes years of practice, determination, and experience—and a little luck—to succeed. There is no magical way to make money quickly. If you take the time to learn and follow your heart with an investment that you like and understand well, you will be able to make wise investment decisions. Be willing to take the time to thoroughly learn all that you can about the investment that you are drawn to. Become intimate with it, try to resonate with it, find the connection with the invest-ment, and see if it is in alignment with your values and goals.

What's Your Comfort Zone with Risk?

Do you hedge your bets? Are you risk-avoidant? Or a reckless risk-taker? Think about the way you handle risk in the various areas of your life: your relationships, business, creative expression. How are you with risk when it comes to managing your money or purchasing things?

Your comfort zone is a place that feels good in your heart

and the rest of your body.

The comfort zone is a feeling of freedom and ease from the pain and discomfort that can result from pushing too hard or being out of touch with what feels good. Of course, growth and development always include some pain and discomfort, and it is usually a part of every human journey until the day we depart from the planet. You can make the decision in your life to stay in your comfort zone or live completely out of your comfort zone or push your edge a bit, stretch out of your comfort zone and see what happens.

If you choose to stay relaxed and content within your comfort zone, you can have a great simple life, but you may not grow and flourish. You may become so risk-averse that you don't push your edge in a way that would be appropriate for your age or financial goals. Sometimes this happens as a result of past setbacks and challenges, which can teach us to be overly cautious and conservative as a reaction. But remember: there is a direct relationship between risk and return. If you are happy with your level of risk and return for where you are at in your life, great. However, if you are healthy and young and can withstand pushing your edge a bit, you will be surprised what will come back to you not just financially, but on other levels as well when you choose to take risks.

In my mid-thirties, I found myself too comfortable and relaxed. I was content with where I was financially, but deep down I was avoiding taking risks that could have been good growth experiences for me, as well as financial assets. I now look back and think "Wow, I could have made 5 to 10 million dollars with a little effort, time, and risk." In the Bay Area and on Maui where these deals were presented to me, the market was rising significantly. Why didn't I go for it? Partly because

I felt I had enough money, and regardless of how much more money I would make, my happiness would not necessarily increase with more money. On the other hand, one could argue that my own courageous risk was to finally say "No, enough is enough," and to be content with what I already had.

Using Money as a Vehicle of Transformation

Staying conscious, embodied, and compassionate around your finances will determine the extent of your transformation as a person. You can use your relationship with money as a tool to gain more insight into your life and your own path of transformation. Making conscious choices around earning, spending, managing, and investing your money in ways that are aligned with your intentions, goals, and financial plan guidelines can be fun and can lead to financial balance. There is no magic way, no shortcut, no true get-rich-scheme. I don't believe in that stuff.

What I can offer you is just the same old reminders over and over. The message stays consistent. The question is: how and what will you do to fully show up in an embodied, openhearted and compassionate way and feel empowered around your money, your job, expenses, debt, and retirement plan? What feelings of joy, peace, and clarity in your heart and body will mobilize you to meet yourself through your finances and at the same time lead to a balanced budget, more income, and more savings?

So when the utility bill arrives and you feel automatic constriction and fear, can you pause and connect with a part of you that feels safe, grounded, and grateful for having the power service to begin with, and hopefully the money to pay for it?

The single rule I want to emphasize (and this rule applies to individuals, families, towns, states, and nations) around creating a budget: Your income must exceed your expenses. It's this simple. If you have money left over, it can be saved or invested, or you can spend it. It's all about choice. But in order to have that choice, you must create a surplus to begin with.

Here is a basic step-by-step plan for establishing structure in your relationship with money in order to arrive at that place.

- **Know how much money you need.** How much money do you need to be comfortable in the short-term and in the long-term? Be realistic. In bountiful times, don't overspend.

- **Have a financial plan.** Make sure it is flexible so it can adapt to changing economic cycles. When we are afraid, we make fear-based decisions. When we are upbeat and happy, we tend to have a more harmonious relationship with money. When you have a sound plan, you won't be dragged around by your emotional mood swings.

- **Plan for the long haul.** Don't worry about the ups and downs of the markets. Plan for five, ten, thirty years from now.

- **Think big.** What you get back financially is in proportion to how much you are open to receive.

- **Pay yourself first.** Despite the ups and downs of the marketplace, make a commitment to pay yourself first—daily, weekly, monthly, or as often as you can. This is a way of investing in yourself, trusting yourself, and not feeding the fear that there will not be enough to go around. This type of discipline and wisdom will build a lot of wealth. If you notice yourself worrying and doubting, stay spacious and compassionate. Stay vigilant and on guard and do not allow yourself to be sidetracked by strong emotions and thoughts.

- **Pay off your debts.** Pay off your debt as fast as you can. Start with the highest interest debts and keep going.

- **Invest with your values.** Make sure your investments are aligned with your ethics.

- **Give.** Be generous. If you have a little, give a little. If you have a lot, give a lot. In this economy it is so important not to sit around being victims and feeling sorry for ourselves. Figure out ways that you can share your gifts with your community. However you can give will be a huge deposit in your spiritual bank account and will open up the door for abundance to flow back to you in unimaginable ways.

SOMATIC EXERCISE: Being Present with Your Checkbook

Are you caught up in a cycle of spending, then regretting it later? Mindfulness can help you by becoming more aware of unwholesome patterns and habits that are no longer serving you. Structure is, unfortunately, something you can't just read about but have to do. Have your checkbook, a notebook, and perhaps your computer ready as you conduct this exercise.

Take out your checkbook register or your bank account or credit card statement and take a few minutes to go through it. Look for places where you can learn a little bit more about yourself. Notice any patterns with your spending? Places where you have "blind spots"? Notice yourself making excuses for things you probably didn't need to buy but can rationalize? Times when you spent too much on something?

Notice how you feel in your body while you are doing this exercise. You can learn a lot about your state of mind and values by looking at your statements. Can you know and accept your financial reality without shame, blame, or judgment?

Often, credit cards allow us to pretend we have more money than we actually have. They can put us in a position of not living in reality and tempt us to make purchases that are not connected to our deeper values.

REFLECTIVE JOURNALING EXERCISE:
Intention Setting

Write a little bit in answer to the following questions:

What do I most deeply want out of this one precious life?

Are my financial choices supporting me in moving closer to what I want? If so, how? If not, why not?

Am I managing my money (earning, spending, investing, etc.) in ways that are causing harm to myself and to others? Or resulting in more peace and abundance for myself and others?

Are my efforts and actions consistent with the way I spend or invest my money? Do they originate from a place of conscious or unconscious fear, greed, constriction, aversion, or denial? Or do they come from a wholesome, generous, loving place of the heart?

Chapter Eight

CREATING A NEW DEFINITION OF PROSPERITY

The real measure of your wealth is how much you'd be worth if you lost all your money.

—Anonymous

The traditional cultural definition of prosperity might be different than our personal one. Just the other day I met a street artist who was colorblind and yet chose to paint for a living. He was semi-homeless, but filled with joy, peace, humor, passion, and creative vigor. When I asked him how he experienced prosperity, he gave me a wise response: "I position myself to be happy, and then share that happiness with others in as many ways as I can, especially through my art." As an artist myself, this was an incredible reminder for me. I consider this homeless street artist to be a teacher, reminding me that happiness is an experience we can decide to have in each moment, and then we can share it with others in whatever way feels good to us. There are so many ways to be prosperous.

Growing up, I remember often thinking, "I want to be happy, free, loved, have friends to play with, a few basic toys, a comfortable home, and decent food." Interestingly enough, after interviewing and observing many people about how they live their lives, I found out that most people want the same things I did as a child (and still do). What differs from one person to the next, however, is exactly how each person defines prosperity and where (and if) they find it in their lives. Through my teaching, I have learned that there are as many special and unique ways to be prosperous, happy, and free from suffering as there are people.

Emily: *Prosperity is about being in the right state of mind. You can be rich even if you don't have money.*

Jim: *Prosperity is gratitude.*

Louie: *I involve myself with people who resonate, who I enjoy, and who support my art. This brings me the greatest joy and prosperity.*

Phoebe: *Prosperity is doing things that make you happy.*

John: *I live on the edge of financial disaster, and yet there is a force that always takes care of me. Even when I'm on my last dollar, I feel held by this force.*

Shakti: *I followed my inner guidance to actualize my creative purpose in life. My attitude is that I am here to share my purpose.*

Prosperity is not a linear thing, a place to go to, or something to get or possess like many of us were taught by society. Rather, prosperity is an experience of being

> **Prosperity is the balance between inner and outer peace, happiness, and material abundance.**

joyfully aware of and gratefully satisfied with the immediate aspects of our life that feed and nourish us.

Even when there is no food to eat or place to sleep, as I discovered in my interviews with the homeless, one can still experience prosperity in one's life. The homeless experience prosperity in their lives in terms of faith, connections with each other, and gratitude for simply being alive. Or they define prosperity as freedom and ease in their lives. This includes lots of free time to express creativity and art, to relax by themselves and with nature and friends, or to simply just be and enjoy each passing moment as it drifts by like the clouds overhead. Being prosperous is not about how rich or poor you are.

What is your personal definition of prosperity? Where do you already have prosperity in your life? Is prosperity just about money, or is it about something more? Perhaps something intangible, like a feeling or an emotional state?

Just the other day, a friend said, "You've been so lucky to have such a prosperous life!" He assumed that the prosperity he was noticing in my life came from magical good fortune. "Not really," I said, laughing. "I don't have any more luck than you have." I gave him the short version of my business education: I grew up around wheelers and dealers, and I've been a businessman all my life—selling seeds door-to-door at age nine, working at various jobs, saving enough money to invest in my first piece of real estate at age eighteen, which turned out to be disaster, and then working hard to save money all over again for my first major development project at age twenty-five, which was another disaster. After going broke a few times, I eventually learned a more conscious, skillful way to live and work, and it all began with deeply reflecting on the question: "What is my intention around the way I work, spend, invest, or share my money?" Slowly gaining clarity around these questions helped me find my way with my finances using clear, achievable goals.

Maslow's Hierarchy of Needs

Like I've said, we all have basic primal needs that are non-negotiable: we all need air, food, water, sleep and shelter. Once those needs are met, we can then start to climb the ladder of having our other needs met: things like friendship, family, sexual gratification, security, self-esteem, and creative fulfillment. Abraham Maslow was a psychology professor in the mid-twentieth century who developed a school of thought called Humanistic Psychology. In his 1943 paper "A Theory of Human Motivation," Maslow posited that, at a base level, we are all motivated by our primal needs, and that in order to grow as humans, those needs must first be met. He introduced the "Hierarchy of Needs" pyramid to show how we ascend from fulfilling our most basic needs to our more highly evolved, self-actualized goals in order to ultimately be successful. He believed that people ascend this ladder in order, from the bottom to the top.

When I first learned about Maslow's Hierarchy of Needs, I saw right away how it applied to my own life. When my family first immigrated to America, we existed at the lowest tier, living

MASLOW'S HIERARCHY OF NEEDS

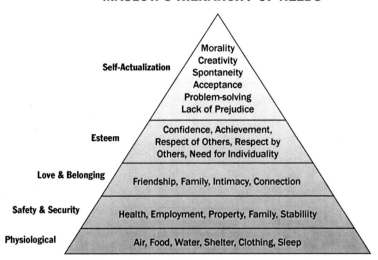

in material poverty and struggling just to eat and pay the rent. We were concerned with our most basic survival needs such as food, water, and sleep. Scared and often insecure, we began to slowly climb the pyramid, and as we did this, we were able to make time and energy for a better quality of life, time together as family, new friendships, leadership roles in community and, most importantly, creative outlets and higher learning.

In my own experience, only when basic economic, physiological, and emotional needs are being met can one feel relaxed enough to have an effective plan to take things to the next level in terms of personal growth. One can meditate all day long, but unless one is actually living in a monastery, it's equally, if not more, important to be generating income to put food on the table. No matter how much praying or meditating one does, money will never fall out of the sky. You can't pay for groceries with karmic points.

The Prosperity Ladder

This Prosperity Ladder can help you make a general assessment of where you are in your financial life. Are you broke and owing money? Or are you relatively comfortable, with a good job? At this early stage, we're not concerned with details like exact income and out-go, or debts and investments. You should simply decide which rung resonates with you. While you are reviewing the Prosperity Ladder, remember that the goal is not necessarily to be at Level 5—at least not yet—but to simply assess where you are and how you will get to the next step.

LEVEL 5
Earning money from accumulated capital

LEVEL 4
Owning or working in a business that makes you money

LEVEL 3
Comfort, a decent job, or stable self-employment but no real wealth

LEVEL 2
Subsistence, just getting by

LEVEL 1
Material poverty, no money, broke

As my own family climbed the Prosperity Ladder, we began to have the emotional security and sense of belonging that comes along with having one's financial needs met. There was a calming effect to having a cash flow and enough money in the bank. I remember my mom having nightmares when I was young and being essentially on the brink of a nervous breakdown as our family hovered between Levels 1 and 2. But she hung in there, and as our real estate business began to grow, her personal growth and sense of fulfillment also expanded. Later, in my own real estate career as an adult, I had a similar experience to the one I saw my mom go through. As I ascended the Prosperity Ladder and Maslow's Hierarchy of Needs through diligent work (and lots of trial and error), I tried not to lose sight of the ultimate prosperity, which was balance in all areas of my life. I was stuck for many years be-

Where are you on the Prosperity Ladder? How about on Maslow's Hierarchy of Needs? Do you see a correlation between the two?

tween levels 1 and 2, just like my mother had been when providing for her family. But the seeds I patiently planted eventually began to sprout.

I believe there can be a direct correlation between financial prosperity and self-actualization if one achieves prosperity in a way that is mindful and authentic. Both financial success and self-growth happen in stages. There are no shortcuts, as far as I know, so it's crucial to be able to stay patiently at whichever stage you are at until the time comes to move up. And "up" is not the only direction to move on the Prosperity Ladder. Often, there will be ups and downs. But in the event that you slide back a level, wouldn't it be great to have the hindsight to be more mindful in each stage? For myself, I know now that even were I to end up back at Level 1 or 2 again, I would have less fear, more patience and would still experience happiness and joy despite my financial situation. I might feel concerned about paying my bills, but I would get by. I live my life knowing that I could potentially have to start all over. This is just how life is. It's a constant ebb and flow when it comes to our money, health, and happiness. But it's important to remember that you can have true prosperity regardless of where you are on the ladder. You can be healthy and peaceful at any stage.

I have to add here that in my work with people across

the spectrum of socioeconomic levels and life circumstances, I have also met plenty of people who had ascended the Prosperity Ladder but were not prosperous in a genuinely fulfilled and spiritual way. I have met plenty of people who lacked in material wealth or even basic comfort, but were content, spiritual, and even sometimes happy. I have also met many people who lived at the top rung of the ladder but lived from a place of fear and basic survival-oriented ways of being.

Maslow believed that human motivation is based on our need for material prosperity in conjunction with personal growth. He described self-actualized people as those who were fulfilled by living up to their potential and expressing themselves to their fullest. He named such legends as Abraham Lincoln, Albert Einstein, and William James as paragons of the self-actualized. I would add to this list Warren Buffet, Bill Gates, Oprah Winfrey, and Steve Jobs. As you evolve and cultivate deeper awareness and mindfulness skills, I urge you to tailor your journey around your own personal dreams and goals.

You Can't Cheat the System

We all often try to jump to the next level on the Prosperity Ladder by borrowing. This enables us to appear more prosperous, with a bigger house or car and more belongings. However, while judicious borrowing may be a good way to increase prosperity, in the long run borrowing beyond your means is a recipe for disaster. In fact, this is one of the causes of the recent financial disaster in this country.

Financial progression means climbing the Prosperity Ladder by working smarter, not necessarily harder. Remember that the goal is to achieve not just material prosperity, but happiness as well. This is accomplished by focusing on all aspects of your life, not just finances. Good physical, emotional, and spiritual health are all necessary to climb the ladder with ease and grace.

Prosperity is really in the eye of the beholder. It is whatever you decide or choose for it to be. Others may have other definitions for themselves, and that's okay. In fact everyone may have a different definition or have a certain image or story they project on the concept of prosperity based on their unique conditioning and culture. Of course, there are those who have doubts or judgments about how some of us view and live with prosperity. Our job is not to change others or waste our energy trying to convince others that we are right, but rather to be an embodiment of prosperity for ourselves, so that our presence inspires the interest and curiosity of others who happen to be in our energetic field of prosperity.

Cultivating a skillful, conscious relationship with money and our friends, co-workers, family members, and partners, and being more skilled in managing stress and anxiety, especially around our finances, will ultimately lead to a more prosperous, abundant life.

It is through living skillfully, with mindful awareness and compassion, that you can achieve unlimited prosperity: money, wholesome relationships, good health, and the ability to respond to life's many challenges by turning them into opportunities for transformation.

REFLECTIVE JOURNALING EXERCISE:
Take an Inventory of Your Current Level of Prosperity

Whatever you have a lot of can be a doorway to deep freedom. Where are you currently experiencing prosperity in your life? Take a few minutes and rate your level or prosperity in the following areas of your life.

- Your emotional, mental, and physical health

- Your family life

- Friends and your social life

- Creativity

- Intimacy and romance

- The satisfaction your derive from your livelihood

- Your financial state

- Your environment

- Your lifestyle

- Spiritual fulfillment

REFLECTIVE JOURNALING EXERCISE:
Where Do You Want To Be?

Now, think about where you would like to make changes.
Dream big. Where would you feel satisfied:

- On the Prosperity Ladder?

- In your work life?

- Geographically?

- In certain relationships?

- Spiritually?

- In terms of your lifestyle?

Write down and date your goals. This will allow you to review them at a future time and assess your progress. Or perhaps you may see that your goals have changed over time. Remember to have fun on your prosperity journey. Keep in mind that you may not be able to stop the waves, but you can learn to have fun riding them.

Chapter Nine

GRATITUDE AND GENEROSITY

When you realize there is nothing lacking, the whole world belongs to you.

—*Lao Tzu*

Gratitude is a powerful instrument for change. It is one of the most direct ways to build up your "prosperity account" and combat money anxiety disorder because it opens you up to become an agent for generosity. The simple act of showing up and being present to yourself and the world, engaging in your community and giving back, and offering kindness and support are the pillars upon which we build our own spiritual bank accounts.

When I was interviewing folks from all walks of life about their unique relationship to prosperity, most expressed their personal experience of prosperity as gratitude for what they had in abundance. In turn, when they focused on what they did have a lot of, a natural response was to feel the urge to give back—money, time, material goods, or even just prayer—and be a more caring, responsible parent, neighbor, friend, or citizen. In this way, appreciation for what we already have leads us to be true leaders in our lives. For me, giving back to the women I teach in the California penal system is a way that I express gratitude for my own financial liberty.

Even in the most challenging settings like the prisons I teach in, those who can be guided back to their heart and to a place of momentary stillness can usually connect with something for which they feel grateful, like simply being alive. We often do exercises to focus in on gratitude. It takes a lot of concentration to support our bad habits. In my workshops, we work on focusing that intense behavior on more productive ways of thinking. We learn Right Concentration. Out of these exercises often come creative, innovative ideas about ways these prisoners can envision leading their lives in the future. I hear things like "I want to give young women the support I never got growing up." Or, "I want to go to vocational school and pursue my dreams." One of my inmate students even dreamed up a pet sitting and grooming business that would be run by released prisoners. These types of ideas are born from a truly grateful place that plants the seeds for later generosity.

But when we get caught up in fear, greed, and constriction, or a narrow-minded view of things, it is easy to forget the relationship between gratitude and generosity. In my twenties, I often forgot about this connection. But my mother never did. Even when we had no money and were scared and down, she would always remind us to find something to be grateful for, no matter how small. Then she would encourage us to practice generosity by showing up for each other. We expressed this is minor ways, like doing chores, making dinner, and always bringing the highest ethics to any job we did.

Where I came from in Iran, the culture encouraged everyone to always appreciate how precious our lives are, how rich our sense of opportunity, how brief our journey on this planet, and how blessed we truly are. As a child, I noticed a lot of generosity being expressed in unison with gratitude, and I felt how it kept our spiritual and economic bank accounts available for rich deposits. Whether rich or poor—or even behind bars—we can always smile at ourselves and others. As new insights begin to emerge and old stories about lack and deprivation begin to fall away, a shift in our core feelings is possible.

Imagine something you are grateful for right now and notice what happens. Often, there is a joyful, mobilizing response to share this feeling of gratitude and abundance. In Chapter Six Impermanence, we talked about how fear arises out of living with ideas of scarcity, greed, and clinging. We also talked about flow. Gratitude and generosity are very important components of a sustainable and joyful flow of abundance and prosperity. The extent of your gratitude often reflects the extent of your generosity, and vice versa. These are interconnected concepts; one feeds off the other. Of course, they are often reflected in the balance of both your spiritual and material bank accounts. These two states of mind are like a noble twofold path that you can choose to walk, regardless of the work you are doing or how much money you have. Mother Teresa is an example of someone who was consistently able to hold gratitude and generosity in the most skillful and humble way, and she became a magnet for gratitude and generosity from all over the world.

Generosity Leads to Prosperity

"If you have a lot, give a lot." This is not just New Age advice, but a tangible philosophy that is embodied by two of the richest men in the world: Warren Buffet and Bill Gates. Both are mindful, engaged, generous, and in the flow with how they run their companies. These two tycoons manage and share their money and time in a way that benefits their shareholders and also humanity.

Warren Buffet has simple taste and a simple philosophy about generosity. He once said that "the perfect amount to leave children is enough money so that they would feel they could do anything, but not so much that they could do nothing.'"

Some of the advice Warren Buffet gives is universal:

- Invest early.

- Don't buy more than what you really need.

- Accomplish things economically. Live your life simply.

- Don't try to show off. Just be yourself.

- Do what you enjoy doing.

- Stay away from credit cards.

- Invest in yourself.

- Remember, money doesn't create the man, but man creates the money.

- Don't do what others say. Just listen and do what feels good to you.

In 2006, when he was the second richest man in the world, Buffet donated 85% of his forty-four billion dollar fortune to a foundation run by the first richest man in the world, Bill Gates, which specializes in finding cures for diseases that plague impoverished nations. The Gates' charity is the largest in the world. Bill Gates transposes the techniques that made his company successful—efficiency, pragmatism, and a dominant position in the market—onto his model of giving. In ten years, the Bill and Melinda Gates Foundation has become a guru in the field of philanthropy.

I also admire Oprah Winfrey a lot, not only because of her ability to connect and engage with her audience, but also because of how she skillfully manages her life and business. She is a model of the American success story, a woman who rose up from a childhood of poverty and lack in the Deep South to become a wealthy and successful national role model and one of the most influential women in the world. Oprah is an incredible model of generosity. Her success proves that regardless of where you are from or what your current socio-economic status might be, you can still rise to the top. Here is something that Oprah once said that I like to share with my students in the jails: "I don't think of myself as a poor deprived ghetto girl who made good. I think of myself as somebody who from an early age knew I was responsible for myself, and I had to make good." This self-responsibility, coupled with a generous and gracious attitude, has propelled her through life and enabled her to provide for herself and those close to her and also to make a real difference in this world.

Loving Kindness

When I give,
I give myself.

—*Walt Whitman*

As a real estate investor in my twenties, I remember getting stuck in mistrust and embroiled in my own usually false negative stories about the tenants in my rent-controlled apartments. I also had limiting beliefs about banks being untrustworthy, attorneys being crooks, insurance companies being evil, and people in general being shifty and dishonest. With this perspective of the world, you can imagine that I didn't feel a lot of gratitude. I didn't see that generosity could be vital to my success. As a result, I experienced much tension, struggle, and the loss of both money and time. Not surprisingly, I was bombarded with lawsuits, maintenance problems, complaints from tenants, and citations from the health department. All of these were out to teach me a lesson.

After a year or so of meditating and looking deeper, I noticed how showing up more generously as a landlord could open up new channels of prosperity and ease for me and everyone else with whom I interacted. I began to use Loving Kindness (metta) meditation techniques in my business dealings. When meditating, I would visualize a person I was struggling with, and I would recite the Metta Mantra.

The Metta Mantra

MAY YOU BE HAPPY.
MAY YOU BE PROSPEROUS.
MAY YOU LIVE WITH EASE AND PEACE

This may sound frivolous, but I noticed an immediate shift. I began to relax and feel a lot more love, forgiveness, and compassion for myself (the first step in a generosity practice) and then for my tenants, the lawyers, and bankers. This opened up channels for even more generosity. In fact, my rental income literally tripled within a few years. I supported my tenants as my most valued customers and did everything possible to express my gratitude for the rent they were paying in exchange for comfortable housing that was affordable. Many eventually came to me for support in buying their own homes. As a result, I kept the cycle of gratitude and generosity going by renting to new folks at market rates. Everyone was a winner. My tenants became homeowners; I was able to raise the rents fairly and legally.

After my first adult experience with "going broke," I gained great insight into my own walls and fears. Gradually, through a regular practice of sitting and being still, I noticed that my motivation to succeed and accumulate more money was rooted in my fears and carried forward in selfish ways in how I interacted with my clients in the real estate business, as well as how I interacted with others. By not pausing to take in the abundance of my life as it was, I had stopped feeling good about myself, and my actions and words reflected this. I was not being sensitive to the needs of others around me. I was consuming too much food and alcohol and felt my survival depended on these external things. This ignorance on my part led to a lot of suffering, loss, and the collapse of my financial life, as well as the disintegration of many precious relationships. When I faced my fears of inadequacy, of not making it or being good enough, I started coming back home to places in my body and heart that had been in a lot of pain.

This homecoming was the initial act of generosity toward myself, and it will be for you as well. It allowed me to begin the first steps on the journey to becoming comfortable in my own skin. I could have just faithfully engaged in selfless acts of service and generosity, despite not being in touch with myself, but sometimes we have to walk a long and hard path before waking up. For me, forgiveness and compassion have been great acts of generosity to myself and others.

The foundational tenet of Buddhist metta practice is that sending even your worst adversaries love and kindness thoughts is a gesture of generosity to yourself. Every time you practice metta, you make a huge deposit in your spiritual bank account. Ideally, this translates to your actual economic bank account as well. When your bank accounts benefit, your heart benefits as well.

Recently I remembered how, as a child, I would be sent around to tenant apartments to collect rent for my mother. I met so many people who all wanted the same thing that my mother and I wanted: happiness, financial independence, health. They couldn't always pay the rent because of the economy or a lack of planning or things simply going wrong in their lives. But I always listened to their stories. We learned to work with our tenants until they could pay. My mom encouraged me to see the human side of every person and every situation, without encouraging bad habits. I still take her advice to heart to this day.

In my personal experience, practicing Loving Kindness, when coupled with an earnest desire to find a win-win solution, led to all of my legal problems being resolved and all of the players in my drama (the tenants, plumbers, electricians, garbage companies, contractors, governments) being able to engage in a lovely exchange of gratitude and generosity that really worked. To this day, I get letters from my tenants expressing thanks for the quality service I have provided them.

Now, let's be honest. No matter how you show up, there will always be those who treat you badly and think you are a jerk. The ultimate practice is to have compassion for even these people, but don't put up with any crap from them, either!

Gratitude, the Great Prosperity Generator

As we express our gratitude, we must never forget that the highest appreciation is not to utter words, but to live by them.

—John F. Kennedy

When we feel grateful for our prosperity, or whatever we have a lot of, there is a homecoming. When we connect with what brings us peace and joy and what we cherish, the natural response is generosity. Gratitude and generosity go hand in hand.

At the other end of the spectrum lies dissatisfaction with what we have, accompanied by avarice. We always want more things. Consumerism encourages us to focus on what we don't have rather than what we do have. As a result, we end up with an emotional handicap. The prime example of this is the materialistic person who believes pleasure and happiness can only be derived from money, status, and possessions. The research shows that such a belief is ill founded and that in many cases the very opposite is actually true. A focus on material wealth is associated with compulsive spending, envy, and low self-esteem. Individuals whose primary focus is affluence and materialism are less satisfied with their life as a whole, tend to experience a higher degree of anxiety and depression, and have a lower sense of wellbeing and more behavioral and physical problems. Some studies have shown that adolescents who highly value material wealth have greater susceptibility to psychological disorders.

The happiness we all seek can only be achieved through

self-enrichment, although of course it's important to have a certain amount of material comfort to support our needs and basic desires.

The Economic Prison of Want

History is rife with stories of greed. Despite the abuse of his name, Epicurus, a Greek philosopher living around 300 BC, encouraged people to enjoy the simple things in life, particularly friends and friendships. He also taught the value of simple foods, from where we have derived the word *epicurean*.

We are conditioned to value money for simply being money. We can easily create an economic prison for ourselves when we think we need more and more and more of it and when we always fear not having enough. Despite our increased wealth over the last thirty years, the rates of divorce, teen suicide, reported violence, and depression continue to increase. Yet our economic and political masters continue to tell us to work harder and buy more to keep the economy going.

But material possessions come and go. The more you have, the more you have to worry about. You work harder and harder, creating an unbalanced life, leaving no time to enjoy the things you really should enjoy, and all of a sudden, you're at the end of your life and you've missed it. I call this deferred living. Wants beget wants. I want, therefore I am... or will be.

The Practice of Skillful Generosity

Skillful generosity allows us to explore and engage in a conscious, revolutionary economic and spiritual model based on voluntary, mindful giving. This is one of the reasons that all Buddhist teachings are provided on a *dana* (donation) basis. The practice of giving is universally recognized as one of the most basic human virtues, a quality that testifies to the depth of one's humanity and capacity for self-transcendence. I recall traveling in Thailand and Laos and seeing the monks going on alms rounds with their bowls empty, ready to receive whatever generosity would come their way by the local villagers who themselves are often very poor. The monks always take what is offered, and the villagers give what they can. The villagers know that the good merits they are creating by supporting the monks cultivate Right Understanding in their own spiritual practice.

In its most simple form, my financial advice to clients always starts with "find a way to give." Regardless of whether you have money or not, be generous.

- **I like the Buddha's rule of thumb about giving:** if you have little, give a little. If you have a lot, give a lot. Avoid being miserly. You can have little in terms of material possessions (like mother Teresa), but still give a lot. You don't have to give money. You can give your time or skills.

- **Random acts of generosity:** Use your skills and resources to help someone you hardly know, or even a stranger. Why? Most of us have something that we are good at, and sharing this with someone outside our immediate circle of friends can make a big impact.

- **Be generous even if you have no money or you are in pain:** Sometimes I feel too empty to be a teacher, but I show up anyway. My students appreciate my showing up and being real, and I appreciate being met by folks that I regard also as my teachers.

I once met an amazing woman who broke her back falling off a horse. She was able to slowly recover, but in the process she lost her job, all her money, and her home. Her biggest comeback strategy when she was able to walk again was to volunteer in her community. Eventually, people recognized her amazing dedication, and she was able to get paid work. Now she is the director of a non-profit organization.

Receiving Is a True Art

In all this talk about generosity, let's not forget about the art of receiving. Being able to gracefully receive the generosity of another is vital in order for prosperity to fully flow back and forth. Some of us are great at giving, but challenged when it comes to asking for support from others. But just as being generous is important to establishing a healthy balance and flow, financially and spiritually, it's important to be able to receive in order to complete this cycle of gratitude and generosity. I know that receiving has been a huge edge for me. It is often a lot harder than giving.

How open are you to receiving? Are you able to ask for what you want and need? Can you feel the pleasure that comes with receiving more money for services performed well? How was the act of receiving modeled by your parents?

Conveniently, when we learn to receive with grace, we experience gratitude, and the cycle is complete. A big part of being able to receive is to have gratitude for what you are given and what you already have regardless of the magnitude of your wealth (or poverty). Observe the wealth you already have in your life. After you have done this, you can then begin to set a few goals toward greater prosperity.

Of course, as with everything in life, balance is the key. You can't just give everything away. But if you step back and look

What are you grateful for in this moment? How generous do you feel right now?

at the big picture of your life you will see how many acts of generosity you might already be participating in without even realizing. The payments you make on bills and rent, the work you engage in, the sunshine and health you receive, the friendships you maintain—these are all actions that require you to give or receive, and sometimes both. You already have the practice. Now it's time to expand your awareness of generosity and gratitude. My wish is that however your life is transformed, you will willingly share your gifts, wisdom, and abundance with others. Whichever way that generosity flows through you is a gift that benefits us all.

REFLECTIVE JOURNALING EXERCISE:
What Are You Grateful For?

Whatever you have a lot of that is increasing your joy, peace, happiness, and comfort also increases your prosperity. So count your blessings! What are you grateful for? Write a list of everything you are currently grateful for in terms of money, material possessions, people, spiritual wealth, or whatever it is. I offer the list below to help jog your memory.

Good health (emotional, mental and/or physical)

Good friends

Close family

A job you enjoy

Passionate creative engagement

Romantic intimacy

Free time

Connection with nature

An ability to stay calm and relaxed despite life's challenges

An ability to stay present with the way things are

Peaceful heart and mind

Appreciation for being alive

Do you have other things to add to this list? You might try spending some time considering this list and your additions to it. What do you already have in your life, and what you would like to have more of? When you decide which areas you would like to enhance, you have begun the process of setting goals. In this process, you will find that the riches you already have will help you to attain your goals. Wealth builds upon wealth.

Take note that financial stability is just one of many components of a rich, happy life. This is what I mean by "putting money in its place."

MEDITATION EXERCISE:
Metta Practice

The basic practice of metta meditation involves repeating
the following lines with heartfelt intention. Sit quietly and
take a moment to just breathe and ground yourself before
you begin. Picture someone in your life that you love. Then,
repeat the following sentences to yourself:

May my life be free from suffering.

May your life be free from suffering.

May all beings be free from suffering.

May my life be filled with peace and prosperity.

May your life be filled with peace and prosperity.

May the life of all beings be filled with peace and prosperity.

*May the flow of money in my life be a reflection of my generosity
and gratitude.*

In the beginning, it might be helpful to write down the mantra
and recite it quietly to yourself during your meditation.
Eventually, you will memorize it.

Typically, in metta meditation, we repeat this cycle, substitut-
ing various subjects for the "you" portion of the prayer. At
first, we picture someone that we are close to and love.
Then, perhaps, we choose someone else who is merely an
acquaintance and who perhaps we feel less emotionally
invested in. Next, we move on to a subject who is a stranger,
perhaps someone whose name we know but who we
have never met. Finally, we choose a subject who is an

emotional trigger for us. It's this last round—sending love and well-wishes to someone who we are not conditioned to love—that is the most powerful aspect of the metta prayer. In this process, we learn that only when we can unconditionally love all of humanity will we ever be truly generous.

MINDFULNESS EXERCISE:
Apply Your Meditation Practice to Your Money

Notice your relationship to generosity when it comes to tipping a server, paying someone for work done for you, or donating money to a panhandler. Without judgment, notice what comes up for you when you are in a situation where you need to make a decision about giving money.

Chapter Ten

DREAM BIG

Whatever you can do or dream, you can begin it. Boldness has genius, power and magic in it.

—Goethe

As immigrants entering into the "American dream," my family felt a strong natural desire to dream big about making it financially and to make a real contribution to our new country, but there were always survival issues to deal with. In addition, we had to contend with our fear of failing, our fear of not being good enough, of not being received and accepted by our neighbors, and naturally this led to a lot of anxiety and stress. Going back to Iran was not an option, so gradually we learned to make it all happen. We were in awe of the unlimited opportunities here in the US—the freedom for anyone to make something happen. This ability to dream was powerful, but thinking back, a lot of it was motivated by fear. Sometimes this fear was legitimate, and sometimes it was imaginary. As much as we were awestruck with the great possibilities, we were often operating mostly from the survival place of fight/flight/freeze.

Like so many families who have lost their homes and

money in the last few years because of the recession, I got a real taste of what it was like to have my dreams threatened by storm clouds of fear, stress, and anxiety because it was hard to find the clarity and safety within ourselves to trust that everything would be okay. And outside of ourselves, we also experienced many ups and downs.

The dreaming wasn't really all that fun until I learned how to dream from a place of joy, trust, and play. Slowly, my family began to have faith and trust that we were safe, that no matter what, the sky was the limit. Learning to be stable within myself—no matter what the world was going through—really made the difference. This is what I love about America: you can choose to be ambitious but stay stuck running on a treadmill, or you can choose to find clarity and balance and define your own version of prosperity (regardless of what the numbers in your bank account look like). You are constrained only by the limitations of your mind and your capacity to be present and attentive to your dreams. If your dream is held by an intention to prosper without greed, selfish motives, or fear, it is truly possible for you to see it come true.

Another immigrant I met through my real estate business, Hanh, had made nine attempts to escape from South Vietnam before he finally boarded a boat with forty other refugees in 1979, hoping to find a better life in the West. After several days of rough seas, they were rescued by a North Korean ship and soon made it to San Francisco, with his father's words ringing in his ears: "Never give up!" He found a job and eventually saved up $25,000, which he invested in a restaurant. Sadly, that restaurant shut down. But he still did not give up. He continued to work and saved money again. He held to his dream, and he never waivered in his Buddhist faith, which emphasizes a gratitude practice as well as a willingness to stay present through suffering and hardship.

By 1984, Hanh was able to buy his first house. In 1995, he bought a second house with a $15,000 down payment. Hanh continued to invest in real estate, and eventually was able to buy apartment buildings and fixer-uppers in San Francisco. He raised two daughters in the US and sent them both to good, expensive colleges. If you ask Hanh what made his good fortune possible in the long run, he will tell you that it was a combination of his Buddhist practice, his faith in God, luck, timing, hard work, and connections. Above all, he will cite his abiding belief that he would make it no matter what. Hanh is now fifty-five years old and worth several million dollars. And he is a genuinely nice person.

Start with a Clear Vision

The future belongs to those who believe in the beauty of their dreams.

—Eleanor Roosevelt

A clear vision supplies the creative energy to speed up your dream's metamorphosis from a tiny seed to a tree bearing abundant, delicious fruit— whether your vision is to earn enough money from work for you to enjoy, save, and invest that money, watch it grow, buy a home, start a business, volunteer your time or to simply become more mindful of how the money flows in and out of your life by creating and abiding by a budget.

Unwavering faith must be the foundation of your dream. I have lost count of how many times my family had to start all over with our finances. Our dream and our vision never changed; we just had to practice taking different approaches to making, investing, and managing money. Because of the economic uncertainty during the various downturns of the '70s, '80s, '90s and the 2000s, we had a lot of opportunities to realize that the journey was in fact our destination. Everything ebbs and flows. Can you still rest the comfort and wisdom of your heart and body in the process as you continue to dream?

As an immigrant, my mother had to stay open to all possible ways of succeeding in this new country, not just financially, but creatively, socially, and spiritually. Often she was thrown off balance as fear, stress, anxiety, and images of doom and gloom clouded her clarity and shook her confidence. But for the most part, she kept dreaming despite several recessions and shake-ups in the real estate market, and, as I grew into an adult, I had a similar experience in my own real estate career. As a result of having a childlike curiosity about the journey I was on, I was able to keep my senses, heart, and mind open and feel what it's like to just sit back and create dreams about the kind of financial reality and quality of living I desired to unfold. It is every immigrant's dream to "make it." You and your ancestors are probably included in this category. In America, most of us are immigrants—if we trace back far enough. Striving to succeed is hardwired into our genetics.

On my own journey to fulfill my big dreams, what was often missing was the energy and passion around my vision that would sustain me through economic ups and downs. I wasn't always so skilled at controlling my emotional reactions to the inevitable change. But as I began inquiring more deeply, using meditation and somatic practices, I learned to hold my clarity of vision and pursue my dream with integrity and by staying true to my own personal values. I thought of myself as a blank canvas, and I sought to paint a picture based on my unique vision.

As a real estate professional I have had the great honor of getting to know Ron Kaufman, one of the most successful real estate developers in San Francisco. Once a janitor, Ron went on to study at UC Berkeley and had a vision to develop urban water properties in our great city. He was able to bring his dream to fruition and eventually wrote a book called *The Old North Water Front: The History and Rebirth of a San Francisco Neighborhood*, which details the history of San Francisco's downtown waterfront as it was settled by the Native Americans, Spaniards, and Mexicans before the statehood of California. A kind, humble family man, Ron has always emphasized teamwork and helpful cooperation with like-minded folks as the keys to his success. He loves his work because it is creative and fun and brings people together around a common theme: reviving San Francisco waterfront properties. For Ron, it's not just about making money. He is truly inspired and considers the revival of San Francisco's historic waterfront his life's work.

I asked Ron for a few pointers on making dreams come true. Here's what he told me:

- **Money doesn't just come from the heavens.** You have to work hard with other like-minded people who share the excitement of your vision. "My vision of converting old waterfront warehouses was good for the city, good for the environment, good for the neighbors, good for the tenants… and good for my pocketbook." This win-win commitment has been crucial to Ron's success.

- **Good communication is a must.** You have to be able to listen just as much as you have to be able to communicate your ideas and visions to everyone involved. Don't be afraid to ask for what you want. Don't hesitate just because you are afraid of hearing a "No."

- **Stay focused on your vision.** Manage your time well. Don't waste time on infighting; don't dwell on negativity; don't be attached to an agenda.

- **Keep things personal.** Reach out and have heart-to-heart contact. Keep the human connection alive.

- **Stay humble.** Never "act rich." Remember where you came from.

- **Give back.** Be generous.

- **Don't focus on the money.** Focus on your creative gift. The money will follow.

My observation of Ron is that he operates much like the billionaire Warren Buffet. He invests with his values and for the long term. He's not out to make a quick buck. I've met many other successful real estate professionals over the years that share Ron's passion and drive for real estate development. Not every real estate developer I meet has the most wholesome of intentions, but I can say that the great majority of the long-term successful developers I know got where they are by staying true to their integrity and vision.

Your Life Is a Blank Canvas

I have been impressed with the urgency of doing. Knowing is not enough; we must apply. Being willing is not enough; we must do.

—*Leonardo da Vinci*

As well as being a real estate investor, teacher, and writer, I am also a painter. So I love the "blank canvas" metaphor. You are a blank canvas. What do you want to create for yourself? How will you take action to execute your personal expression or dream? When you imagine your life as a blank canvas, what would you like to paint on it? What colors, shapes, shades, lines, and images speak to you? You can create whatever you want! What image of the "Life Masterpiece" would you like to create in this one short life? We are not here on this planet for very long. Since we are not going to be alive forever, what are some steps you can take now to create your dream life? I'm not talking about merely achieving a sustainable level of satisfaction and joy in your life. I'm talking about offering your unique gift to the world so that others can have a chance to grow and prosper as a result or your contribution. It's never too late.

A colleague of mine, Joan, started meditating at the age of eighty and, after attending many retreats, had a deep realization that her blank canvas should be filled with charity efforts.

She funded and developed a community mindfulness center to support members of her community suffering from severe trauma: vets returning from Afghanistan and Iraq with PTSD and single mothers facing homelessness. I was blessed to be able to take part in her efforts. Through her center in San Francisco, I teach a monthly Mindfulness & Money course and invite the community to attend on a sliding scale donation basis.

Money as a Blank Canvas

Money sometimes gets a bad rap. It's only a tool, a medium of exchange. You can't eat it or build a house with it. Whatever you project onto it is what tends to materialize, grow, and get carried forward in how you spend it, invest it, earn it, and share it. If your projections about money include lack, fear, stress, anxiety, greed, or constriction, expect your journey to be bumpy and turbulent, regardless of how much money you have.

I often coach my clients on how to approach their blank canvas. Here are some things to consider as you approach your own.

- **Have fun.** Play and enjoy the journey. Allow for your inherent childlike curiosity to unfold and express itself without judgment. It's in being in the spirit of playfulness, joy, and fun that most of best paintings are created. Pause often and check in to see if you are really having fun and to reconnect with yourself— body, mind, heart, and head. If you find tension, then you need to take another approach. Find and follow the joy, not the fear.

- **Practice being generous and helping others to realize their dreams.** I do this in my Mindfulness & Money classes and in working with men and women in jail whose own dreams have been shattered. There is something magical about the act of giving, however unique the way in which it comes from you: perhaps simply the generosity of a smile, your presence, or a listening ear.

- **Feel and speak your dream.** What is the feeling tone of your dream? Is it fuzzy, velvety, smooth and silky, or is it rough, heavy, dense? Trust this deeper wisdom of your body. It never lies. Allow every word you speak to reflect your dream.

- **Feel prosperous.** Focus on what you are grateful for! Refer back to the list you made at the end of the last chapter on gratitude and generosity.

- **Avoid scarcity and limited thinking.** If you notice yourself going into limited thinking mode or fixating on scarcity, pause, take a few deep breaths, connect with your body, and feel the abundance of support that is keeping you alive right now: the oxygen, the lungs that take it in and out, the heart pumping millions of gallons of blood every week, the earth that provides for you, and the sun above. Why would you get stuck in limitation when the world we live in is so abundant?

- **Be spontaneous and improvise if you have to.** I actually involve my students in a lot of theatre games and improvisational exercises during my workshops to get them to engage with life in silly, fun ways that the mind isn't used to understanding. The results are astounding. There are often insights about money, work, and skillful ways to live.

- **Have unwavering faith.** Expect change! Everything will ebb and flow, but your faith doesn't ever have to waiver. Always simply get back on track and hold a steady course toward your financial goals, even if you sometimes get thrown off course.

Define Your Vision

Your vision begins with the seeds of the intentions you want to plant in the soil of your heart. Goals are a way of creating a plan to get there.

Your vision represents the scope and the foundation of your dreams, and it must be a sharp and clear picture of what you want, especially with your finances. When I paint, before I put anything onto the canvas, I have a vision of what I want to create. I sketch it out, research the scale and scope, define the message I want to share, and anticipate the reactions I hope to evoke in the viewer. I approach my financial life in the same basic way. I plan ahead: what do I want my financial life to look like in a year? Five years? Twenty-five? How do I want it to feel? No matter where I am at in my life, I keep my vision focused about what I ultimately want to create. If I find myself wandering off my path, I simply recognize what is happening and readjust. This is the mindfulness practice.

Just like when you notice your mind going off into a story, if you notice your dreams losing their vividness, or your vision becoming cloudy, it's time to look back at your original plan. Gently and compassionately pause; take a breath; reconnect with the belly, hands, and feet; and take a quick look at the reality of what is going on. Then, ask yourself: "Am I safe right now? Is everything okay in this moment?" If the answer is yes, then acknowledge that it's safe and okay to take a step forward toward realizing my financial dreams. Just one step. One breath. One moment at a time. There are no shortcuts.

Take Action to Achieve Your Financial Goals

Skillful, balanced effort provides the energy required to take action to achieve and sustain a successful financial life. It takes diligent and focused cultivation of skillful means to achieve your financial dreams. If you don't stay mindful of your financial target and stay in tune with your deeper motivation, or if you waiver or lose focus of what you want to create, you can find yourself with unwholesome outcomes. You must make the effort to take action to achieve your financial and life dreams with integrity, stay aware and focused, and try to find a balance between under-effort and over-effort.

As a part of the practice of staying aware and focused, pause often in your daily life—while paying bills, during a job interview, while on a sales call, during a presentation—to check in with yourself. Notice your posture, your tone of voice, your connection to yourself and others. Are you relaxed, or stressed? Are you leaning forward with your body, or back? Is your belly relaxed, or tensed? Just naming what is going on is physically is often enough to bring us back to realignment: tingling in my hands and feet, tension in my jaw or shoulders, constriction in my belly feels like this! Name your state of mind and emotion: frustration, anxiety, worry, sadness, greed, confusion. Make a mental note.

If one is to succeed in anything, the success must come gently. With a great deal of effort. But with no stress or obsession. Be vigilant, alert, and aware, and if you notice the symptoms of stress, this means it's time to pause, check in, and regroup.

REFLECTIVE JOURNALING EXERCISE: Dream Big

What do you want your financial life to look like in six months?

A year?

Five years?

How can your vision serve to inspire and motivate you and others to dream dreams and take skillful actions that can transform you and the planet?

What qualities and values will you embody in your vision?

How does it look and feel to hold a vision of what you want?

CREATIVE SOMATIC EXERCISE: Draw Your Dream

Find a comfortable place to sit or lie down. Close your eyes.
Take a few breaths. Put one hand on your heart and one
on your belly. Now, imagine your financial future. Just like a
movie on a movie screen, give yourself permission to allow
your imagination to flow visually. Notice with compassion
the sensations, thoughts, and reactions that come up in this
exercise.

Now, grab your journal or a blank piece of paper. Imagine that
you yourself are a blank canvas. A financial genie comes to
visit you and says you can have any money wish come true.
What is your wish? Be specific. (Don't just say, "I want a
million dollars.") Describe your wish in terms of color, shape,
and feel. Use colored pencils or markers to draw and paint it.

CONCLUSION

There is a new financial paradigm beginning to take shape in the world. This paradigm includes greater generosity, more knowledge, less greed, and a mindful stewardship of Earth's resources. It grows stronger and more vital each time someone chooses to leave old ways of thinking behind and prioritize happiness and true prosperity from the heart.

The old paradigm placed money at the top and equated more money with greater happiness. But this way of thinking can, paradoxically, bring a great deal of imbalance and unhappiness by causing us to feel a collective money anxiety. In our quest for more and more money, we run the risk of ignoring our families and friends and the things that really matter. The greed inherent in this paradigm brought on an epidemic of money anxiety disorder and, ultimately, the economic recession of 2008–2009.

I embodied Money Anxiety Disorder for a long time in my own life, and I am intimately familiar with its causes and effects. I still have to deal with occasional waves of temptation around greed and aversion; this seems to be an inherent part of my constitution. But staying compassionate and spacious as the waves come and go and consistently practicing the art of generosity and giving back seems to balance me out. I notice the constriction that comes with unmindful tendencies, and I consciously release them when I take a moment to reconnect with the reality around me.

By placing happiness, peace, and joy at the top of our priority list, we relegate money to its proper place: a means to an end, equal to all of the other components of a happy life. Embracing this equation places us squarely in the new paradigm of a sustainable, balanced financial life and banishes money anxiety disorder to the past.

The New Economic Paradigm

If we could change ourselves, the tendencies in the world would also change. As a man changes his own nature, so does the attitude of the world change towards him. We need not wait to see what others do.

—*Gandhi*

Our old economic paradigm lacked embodied awareness. We saw how cycles of greed and corruption resulted in the bankruptcy of our material and spiritual bank accounts. But we also saw how they gave us the opportunity to meet our many teachers and find our way back home. As we begin to transition from the old paradigm to a new way of relating to our financial circumstances, there will not, I'm afraid, be a magic answer or a one-size-fits-all path, nor will there be any shortcuts to getting rid of challenges and uncertainty. Just like a wise investment takes time to grow over time, our consciousness and our heart's capacitys must develop through patient training and practice. We have to show up moment by moment and slowly peel away each successive layer of conditioning until we have shed our old story completely. I know that this is possible because I myself have done it. I let go of my old story, my built-in tendency to panic about money, my go-to mechanism of shutting down emotionally, and my habit of living from a perpetual state of fear-based survival response. I learned to calm my nervous system and developed a more centered approach to dealing with my finances. It's still and will always be an ongoing, day-to-day practice. But I now have the tools at my disposal. Two of the most important tools for me are generosity and service. For you, there might be other tools.

Back when I was caught in the web of greedy thoughts about making easy money by preying on vulnerable and desperate property sellers, my somatic response was like a lion in the savannah chasing gazelles. My reptilian brain was in control of my behavior and decision-making until it was interrupted, fortunately, by the collapse of the economy and my net worth. But you don't have to wait until this happens to you. You can be proactive and learn to tune in to your body, your heart, and your checkbook with a mindfulness practice. You can begin to see your breath as the great metaphor of how energy must flow in and out of your life without struggle or constriction.

As I reflect back on my own financial life journey, I feel compassion for my former self and others who may not be consciously aware of their deeper motivations. In the same way, I feel compassion for my teenage daughter when she makes choices that are not exactly skillful. When she becomes greedy and obsessed about playing games on her iPod, I will ask her to pause and take a breath. Often, she resists or rebels. But when I suggest other alternatives, such as going for a walk or playing a board game with me, more often than not she will put the gadget down and make a different choice. In her old paradigm, she was staring into a little electronic box all day, participating as the ultimate consumer slave, losing contact with herself and her family. The somatic results were obvious: hunched shoulders, tight jaw, dilated pupils—signs of stress, basically. The new paradigm she creates when she puts down the iPod is about community, fun, joy, and interaction.

As I have done "the work" over the last decade, I have begun to feel very different in my own body. I have surrounded myself with caring and prosperous individuals who support me. I know this is a reflection of where I am in my life. On occasion, I get frustrated and edgy, just like everyone else. But because this is not my normal way of being anymore, those who surround me in my community can stay patient, kind, and tolerant when I act this way. When we care about people and trust them, we hold a big space for them, even when they occasionally wander off the path.

Creating Community Support

My advice to you: find a community you can resonate with. Create a social network of kind, clear, openhearted people who care about you, what you are doing, and what you are offering the world. Seek the support of people wiser than you so you can grow and learn from them. Don't stay in the comfort zone with negative people who don't share your life and money values. Stay away from folks who are not conscious about their spending or who have limited consumer values. Unless these people are committed to making a conscious shift, hanging around them will drag you down.

People who are in resonance with each other and share values and goals are naturally drawn together. This is how great communities are formed. This is true whether we are talking about the romantic partners we choose, the friends we surround ourselves with, the associates we do business with, the support groups we attend, or the advisors we elect. When your values are based on achieving win-win prosperity for everyone, then you attract the support of folks who are aligned with them. If, on the other hand, you are aligned with a win-lose, fear-based greed model, you will attract like energy.

I started my Mindfulness & Money courses to share my own experiences with others and also to create a community forum from which I could gain support. For these same reasons, I enjoy sharing my knowledge of money and mindfulness with others through my blog and this book. Perhaps there is a community support group in your area that you can join in order to share your own experiences and values with like-minded citizens. If not, consider starting one yourself!

My wish for you is that as you go forward on the path, you will make choices that are based on Right Intention and your highest, heart-based values, choices that create goodness and abundance for all. When our financial choices come from a place of caring and love, as well as from an anchored place in our bodies, then we have the potential to create and spread more caring, love, and mindfulness in the world.

Recommended Reading

Think and Grow Rich by Napoleon Hill (2013)

Natural Capitalism: Creating the Next Industrial Revolution by Paul Hawken, Amory Lovins and L. Hunter Lovins (2008)

The History of Money by Jack Weatherford (1998)

The Oracle Speaks: Warren Buffett In His Own Words (In Their Own Words) by David Andrews (2012)

Your Money or Your Life: 9 Steps to Transforming Your Relationship with Money and Achieving Financial Independence: Revised and Updated for the 21st Century by Vicki Robin, Joe Dominguez and Monique Tilford (2008)

Buddha's Brain: The Practical Neuroscience of Happiness, Love, and Wisdom by Rick Hanson and Richard Mendius (2009)

The Soul of Money: Reclaiming the Wealth of Our Inner Resources by Lynne Twist and Teresa Barker (2006)

Mindfulness and Money: The Buddhist Path of Abundance by Dominic J. Houlder and Kulananda Houlder (2003)

Financial Recovery: Developing a Healthy Relationship with Money by Karen McCall and John Bradshaw (2011)

The ABCs of Money by Natalie Pace (2012)

The 7 Habits of Highly Effective People by Stephen R. Covey (2004)

A Path with Heart: A Guide Through the Perils and Promises of Spiritual Life by Jack Kornfield (1993)

Resources

Palmer, Nancy. "5 Ways to Cope with Money Stress." *O The Oprah Magazine*. Mar. 2009. http://www.oprah.com/money/5-Ways-to-Cope-with-Financial-Stress-and-Anxiety (4 Mar. 2013)

Holt, Doug. "The Role of the Amygdala in Fear and Panic." Jan. 8, 2008. http://serendip.brynmawr.edu/exchange/node/1749 (4 Mar. 2013)

greed. 2012. In Dictionary.com. Retrieved March 4, 2012, from http://dictionary.reference.com/browse/greed?s=t&path=/

His Holiness the Dalai Lama and Howard D. Cutler, M.D. (2009). *The Art of Happiness: A Handbook for Living* (10th ed.). New York: Riverhead Books.

Maslow, Abraham. (1943). "A Theory of Human Motivation." Psychological Review, 50, 370-396. http://psychclassics.yorku.ca/Maslow/motivation.htm (4 Mar. 2013)

Luscombe, Belinda. "Money Buys Happiness When Income Is $75,000." *Time*. Sept. 6, 2010. http://www.time.com/time/magazine/article/0,9171,2019628,00.html (4 Mar 2013)

Staff. Woodrow Wilson School of Public and International Affairs Princeton University "Income's Influence on Happiness." http://www.princeton.edu/news/Income_Happiness/ (4 Mar. 2013)

Huntington Outreach Project for Education at Stanford. "Meditation and HD." Posted in *Lifestyle* and *HD*. June 26th, 2010 https://www.stanford.edu/group/hopes/cgi-bin/wordpress/2010/06/meditation-and-hd/ (4 Mar. 2013)

Loomis, Carol J. "Warren Buffet Gives it Away." *Fortune*. Jul. 13, 2006. http://money.cnn.com/magazines/fortune/fortune_ archive/2006/07/10/8380864/index.htm(4 Mar. 2013)

Kirkland, Richard I., Jr. "Should You Leave It All to the Children?" *Fortune*. September 29, 1986. http://money.cnn.com/magazines/ fortune/fortune_archive/1986/09/29/68098/index.htm (4 Mar. 2013)

Moffitt, Phillip. "The Heart's Intention." *Yoga Journal*. Sept./Oct. 2003. http://www.yogajournal.com/wisdom/926 (4 Mar. 2013)

ABOUT THE AUTHOR

K oorosh Ostowari is the founder and president of Prosperity Today, an organization dedicated to the practice of mindfully cultivating and maintaining balance and prosperity in everyday life. For the past five years, he has offered *Mindfulness & Money* courses throughout the San Francisco Bay Area, offering tools to help clients learn how to integrate their spiritual and material lives in order to attain prosperity in both. He is a Spirit Rock Meditation Center trained community Dharma Leader, a certified somatic therapist, and a spiritual and communications teacher for incarcerated men and women at a Northern California jail.

Koorosh also has twenty-five years of experience operating a very profitable real estate business in San Francisco. In his own life, he has successfully bridged the gap between spiritual and material riches. His goal is to share the mindfulness and somatic tools he's learned with others through this book.

Contact Koorosh Ostowari

For further information on this book, workshops, classes, and speaking engagements, you can contact Koorosh at: *koorosh@themoneyanxietycure.com.* You can also contact and connect with Koorosh here:

Website: *TheMoneyAnxietyCure.com*
Facebook: *facebook.com/PersonalProsperityToday*
Twitter: *twitter.com/MindfulMoney1*

CPSIA information can be obtained at www.ICGtesting.com
Printed in the USA
BVOW01s1815241013

334593BV00001B/3/P

9 781939 116369